Fashion in the '70s

Emmanuelle Dirix
&
Charlotte Fiell

Published in 2014 by Goodman Fiell

An imprint of the Carlton Publishing Group

20 Mortimer Street, London W1T 3JW

www.carltonbooks.co.uk

A CIP catalogue record for this book is available from the
British Library.

ISBN 978-1-78313-010-8

Introduction and chapter opener text © 2014 Emmanuelle Dirix

Captions and biographies © 2014 Carlton Books Ltd

Design © 2014 Carlton Books Ltd

Printed in China

Fashion
in the '70s

Emmanuelle Dirix
&
Charlotte Fiell

GOODMAN
FIELL

Contents

Opposite
Actress and model Lauren Hutton wearing a long pale pink slashed halter-neck
gown, 1971 – accessorized with chunky grey and pink shell bangles by David
Webb. This photograph by Bert Stern was featured in the November 1971 issue
of American *Vogue*. As a top fashion model appearing on the cover of American
Vogue a record 26 times, Lauren Hutton was seen as "the fresh American face
of fashion" during the late 1960s and throughout the '70s

Introduction Seventies fashion
The decade that taste forgot?

The Seventies is a decade that is, for many, somewhat of a conundrum: for those who were there, it often represents a period that is looked back at with humorous and often apologetic embarrassment, while for those who weren't it is romanticized as the last decade of relative freedom and free love before the onslaught of Eighties yuppie culture and the glorification of greed and wealth. Most often, though, especially with regards to fashion and style, it is known as the decade that taste forgot.

In 1980, Christopher Booker in his book *The Seventies: Portrait of a Decade* pondered, "what will in years to come evoke the sober gloomy seventies … what was the seventies look?"[1] His answer suggests that there would be no recognizable style that defined the decade. Of course, it is always difficult to reflect on the immediate past and deduce coherent or accurate conclusions, but not only did he believe that there was nothing special about Seventies style, he went on to state that in years to come it would be unlikely to be a time that would inspire us or fill us with nostalgia. From today's perspective, we see that nothing could be further from the truth: we need only to look at the latest upcoming spring/summer catwalk collections (and indeed their watered-down versions in high street stores) to see the clear influence of Seventies maxi dress, peasant and hippy styles.[2]

But while Booker had the excuse of writing just as the decade had drawn to a close, what could justify the dislike for the era's styles that is upheld by many other writers, journalists and cultural critics to this day? In 1988, John Savage made the canny observation that our reaction to Seventies fashion is a result of conditioning

rather than a true consideration of the styles which he said by the 1980s had become "directly associated with attributes that have no place in Success Culture".[3] The air of freedom and the anti-institutional ethos that was part of so many of the decade's fashions was indeed in stark contrast with the aggressive branding and logo culture of the Eighties.

This may explain why recently we've seen a revival of Seventies styles as contemporary culture not only faces similar issues to those experienced in the late 1970s – in particular in the economic and political domains – but there is also the spreading awareness that our current problems are a direct result of wheels put in motion in the 1980s. Ultimately, "Success Culture" proved to be a lie, evidenced by the collapse of the banking system. The resulting global recession's impact has resulted in hardships comparable to those experienced in 1970s. Equally a contemporary growing engagement with eco-politics means that similar issues and concerns are central to both decades' discourse and this is reflected now, as it was then, in popular fashion styles.

Indeed, while fashion is often accused of being nothing more than superficial, empty and fetishistic – which it can of course be – it does in fact also provide us with a lens through which to view and "read" society. Or, as the cultural commentator Daniel Roche puts it, "fashion is the most talkative of social facts".[4] By putting value judgements aside and instead looking at the various sartorial symptoms of a specific time without subjective emotive considerations, we can read what lies beneath the surface: a society's hopes and aspirations but also its fears and anxieties – fashion is,

Above
Model wearing a colourful machine-knitted zigzag and
striped outfit by Missoni and posing on pillows also covered
in Missoni fabric, 1975

Opposite
Multi-coloured Acrilan knit vest worn with a yellow silk shirt, a
gored printed skirt, red mohair hat and amber beads by Ginger
Group, 1975 – the Ginger Group label was established by
Mary Quant in 1963 and was used for a line of clothing that
was more affordable than her signature collections

after all, created by the circumstances in which it has
to operate.

Whereas Savage's notion that we dislike the
Seventies because we were taught to do so goes
some way to explaining why many have such an
extreme reaction to anything to do with the decade,
there are, however, a few other notions that need to
be considered. In cultural terms the Seventies is often
remembered as a time of crisis and confusion: it is seen
as a decade that was edging forward yet constantly
looking back. The many, often contradictory, popular
fashion styles of the decade are often used to justify
this assumption. However, as will be discussed later,
this is not necessarily the correct translation, nor the
only reading, of the language of Seventies fashion. The
fact that there were so many different fashion styles to
choose from has led to the idea of choice being read
as confusion and as such has contributed to the idea
there is no such thing as a discernable Seventies look.
In many ways this latter assumption is quite true: there
was no *one* look that defined the era, there were many.
But to use this fact to conclude that Seventies style
was non-existent is oversimplifying matters and by
extension reducing a decade – which arguably created
the blueprint for our contemporary "supermarket of
styles"[5] high street – to one with little new or exciting
to offer.

This leads to another factor that needs
consideration: excess. The many different styles
popular during the period not only resulted in many
concluding that the time lacked a clear coherent course,
it also led the decade to be seen as one of excess.
Excess is, of course, a very ambiguous term, as it must
always be considered in relation to something clearly
less excessive. In the case of Seventies fashion, this
would be Sixties fashion, as one can only compare an
era to one that has gone before. In fact, if we compared
the number of styles worn during the Seventies with,
say, the first decade of the twenty-first century, the
word "excess" would hardly apply as we go through
fashionable styles at a faster rate than ever before.

Certainly, the Sixties had witnessed a veritable
design revolution, which saw youth fashions move in a
very different direction to the course taken by Parisian

Haute Couture (an industry which although in financial
decline still proved a force to be reckoned with), but in
retrospect it offered less than a handful of key looks.
The most famous of these is the mini skirt, which must
be considered the last truly universal fashion in that
the majority of women took it up, albeit gradually. In
comparison, the availability of fashion choices in the
Seventies with its plethora of styles and looks could
therefore be considered excessive. This abundance
of choice, paired with the fact it was also a time of
economic hardship, naturally only compounded its
reputation as a time of bad taste; for novelty and "The
New" are considered superficial and wasteful even
in the best of times. Again this raises the question of
whether this bad taste judgement is actually based on a
consideration of the actual garments or what they were
perceived to represent?

The term "New" also needs closer attention when
trying to ascertain the roots of the ongoing hostility
against the era's style and in particular the accusation
that it had nothing novel to offer. The Seventies was the
first decade to embrace on a mass scale what we would
now define as retro-looks. While in previous decades
elements from historic fashion had resurfaced (e.g. in
1909 Paul Poiret re-introduced the Empire waistline, and
The New Look of 1947 saw Christian Dior borrowing
1850s elements), in the Seventies this historic borrowing
was taken to new heights. Rather than using history
as inspiration for the creation of new designs, the past
was now more closely copied, albeit in a distinctive
and romanticized manner. From Biba's slinky 1930s
Hollywood glamour dresses to Laura Ashley's pastoral
Edwardian milkmaids, the past came to dominate the
Seventies wardrobe.

Does this mean that these fashions had nothing
new to say? Arguably in terms of design they were less
"original" than previous fashion movements, but this
mass adoption of historic costume in itself was original
and new, and very much a product of circumstance.
Equally this historic pillaging once again paved the
way for the retro fashions that now each season take
up large parts of designer and high street collections.
The borrowing was not just limited to times past (or, as
we'll see, times imagined) but also extended to foreign

cultures, and most radically to the borrowing between genders; throughout the decade women almost universally adopted what had previously been regarded as men's styles, but equally male wardrobes, some would argue for the first time since the early nineteenth century, also became more feminized.

This abundance, or excess, of fashionable styles (let alone individual items) makes it difficult if not impossible to create a book that covers each and every one. Hence, instead of even attempting such a doomed-to-fail undertaking, this volume aims to present a cultural overview of Seventies fashions that will identify the major stylistic changes and movements rather than provide a long list of all things fashionable. Furthermore, it will contextualize and locate these in a wider discourse about the decade to demonstrate how fashion is at once a barometer of culture and often the location where unresolved and contested social

and political ideas take shape and find expression. It also aims to dispel the negativity associated with 1970s fashion and change its popular narrative of confusion and lack of direction to one that celebrates this decade as a time that glorified consumer choice and individuality and ushered in a truly modern democratization and individualization of style.

Fashion historian Maryléne Delbourg-Delphis[6] has noted that prior to 1963, women automatically followed fashion. She stated that this attitude changed during the 1960s as (youth) fashions shook people up and forced them to accept more fantastical styles, but that it was only in the 1970s that public opinion rendered fashion "optional" and personal choice truly ruled. For this reason Seventies styles are sometimes referred to as anti-fashions.

The phrase "anti-fashion" is now often used by academics and the fashion press alike to describe

Women's Country Casuals – seated: doll-printed blouse worn with a mint-green pinafore apron and green corduroy cuffed pants from Macy's and a violet printed aqua smocked camisole and pants by Betsey Johnson; standing: flower-sprigged ecru and black gauze dress from The Emporium in San Francisco, white dotted smock outfit by Betsey Johnson, and a muslin and calico frontier dress from City of Paris department store in San Francisco, 1973

the latter half of the decade and more precisely the shocking and often outwardly aggressive subcultural punk styles that emerged during this period. While these were very much overtly and spectacularly anti-fashions (in the sense that they countered established norms of beauty and elegance, at which punk not only turned up its nose up but effectively spat), this is a one-sided and extreme interpretation of anti-fashion.

The first half of the 1970s saw equally spectacular, albeit less shocking, styles, which could also be termed as anti-fashions. The most important thing to recognize from the outset is that the plethora of available fashionable styles – which, as discussed, was seen by many as a form of chaos without direction – can in fact be read as a symptom of the fact that Fashion (with a capital "F") was simply not *in fashion*.[7] Since the seventeenth century, Paris had been the centre of all things fashionable and tasteful. With the establishment of the Haute Couture industry in the latter half of the nineteenth century, its reputation as a fashion dictator was cemented and underpinned by a successful creative business endeavour: what Paris created those in fashion wore. Practically this resulted in a system that saw the elite from all over the world travel to the city twice a year to be educated about what would be fashionable in the season to come. For those of lesser means but with aspirations to fashionability, copies of the Parisian styles (either licensed or counterfeited) were available in department stores on both sides of the Atlantic. Local "designers", couture houses and dressmakers all took their cue from Paris and this resulted in a top-down system where only something that had originated in the salons of the Haute Couturiers was considered Fashion. Anything else, however elegant or quaint, fell outside this categorization.

From the late 1950s, young designers, particularly in London, had started challenging if not rejecting this Parisian dominance and had instead started creating their own styles. A generation of young entrepreneurs with a thirst for difference and novelty fuelled London's boutique boom and introduced not only a new shopping experience but also more importantly a new look – or a variety of looks, to be precise – that allowed young

people to dress differently from their parents and thus outwardly display their individuality and identity.

These boutiques, such as Bazaar by Mary Quant, Biba, I Was Lord Kitchener's Valet, Hung On You, Granny Takes a Trip and many others, retailed either second-hand (or "antique" as they preferred to call them) garments or new original designs, or a mixture of both. The clothes they sold and the looks they promoted, regardless of their originality, could not wholly be considered Fashion as their popularity and indeed their dissemination was limited to a young, urban hip crowd. However, by the second half of the Sixties, elements from these alternative modes of dress had started bubbling up into mainstream fashion, most notably the mini skirt, and designers worldwide started (often grudgingly) taking note of what was happening on the street.

The boutique ethos soon spread to Paris, where young designers such as Sonia Rykiel and Karl Lagerfeld – referred to as "yé yé"s after The Beatles' refrain in their 1964 hit "She Loves You" – married innovative and young design with Parisian chic. Paris, aware of this threat to its position as the arbiter of taste, reacted in varying ways: while more conservative houses saw these youth fashions as nothing more than vulgar attention-seeking, some more visionary and often younger couturiers understood that if Haute Couture was to survive, things had to change. This change came through the introduction of *prêt-a-porter* collections, which by doing away with the multiple fittings required for Haute Couture garments had a consequently lower price tag, which was meant to attract a younger audience.

Since 1945, Haute Couture had been financially struggling owing both to the problematic decisions made by the industry during the Second World War and to the emergence in the aftermath of the war of ready-to-wear clothing that was of increasingly better quality and also better designed. Yet even though its clientele had massively declined, Haute Couture's position as the world leader of fashionable taste had not waned concurrently. Nevertheless, no business can survive on prestige alone, which is why Yves Saint Laurent decided that new strategies were needed to rejuvenate the industry. So he opened his *prêt-a-porter* house YSL

Right
British model Twiggy wearing a long black
sequined dress with matching arm-warmers
accessorized with a close-fitting black
turban, chunky necklace, red tights and high-
heeled red suede shoes by Biba, 1971 – this
photo shoot by Justin de Villeneuve was
taken in Biba's Art Deco-themed Kensington
store

Oppposite
Long knitted jumper dress
worn over a turtleneck
and a shirt, top and long
skirt ensemble by the San
Francisco-based designer
Paul Maris, 1972

Above
Actress Elaine Elder wearing a
striped red and green pullover,
a long red and yellow knit gilet,
white shorts and white leather
platform boots, 1972

Oppposite
Opposite
Dr Aldo Gucci shown in the Gucci store on Michigan Avenue, Chicago with two models wearing examples of his latest collection, 1972 – to the left, a jacquard wool skirt with a classic Gucci horse-bit-and-harness trim worn with a fine wool shirt, and to the right, a white knitted evening skirt with navy banding worn with a matching shawl and a navy turtleneck sweater

Rive Gauche in 1967. The clothes on offer in his ready-to-wear collection were not a watered-down version of his Haute Couture offerings, instead he presented clothes that clearly took their inspiration from young street fashions. The Couture establishment initially reacted with horror, but Rive Gauche soon turned out to be a financial stroke of genius and others jumped on the bandwagon. The success of *prêt-a-porter*, which is effectively a diffusion line that exploited the cultural status of Haute Couture to promote (relatively) cheaper fashions, meant that a wider range of fashionable styles now became available to choose from. By associating a couture name with what were essentially upmarket ready-to-wear youth fashions, Saint Laurent gave individuality and diversity the Paris seal of approval and so turned what had previously been the exclusive domain of young hipsters into mainstream fashions.

In 1971, Yves Saint Laurent declared to *Elle* magazine that from now on he would concentrate on *prêt-a-porter* as his true public consisted of young women who worked, and that couture would last for only another five more years or so[8] – a clear put-down of an industry and system that was now considered outdated even by those on the inside. This shift constituted a major cultural change and reflects the growing feeling by the start of the 1970s that fashion was no longer about fitting in with a system but about personal freedom and the expression of individuality. In 1972 *The Evening Standard* stated that they wouldn't "be spending any more time reporting the funeral obsequies of a moribund institution"[9] and Kennedy Fraser in 1975 echoed this sentiment, albeit somewhat more aggressively, when he declared that Haute Couture was a degenerate institution propped up by a sycophantic press.[10]

Others, rather than attacking the Haute Couture industry, focused on the positive outcomes of its decline and diversification. In 1976, Clara Pierre decreed, "Let us grant to the seventies its claim to antifashion, for the freedom to wear what you want, where and when you want, is finally here."[11] Even *Vogue* in the early 1970s declared, "There are no rules in the fashion game now." *Vogue*, part if not central to what Fraser termed the sycophantic press, was one of many fashion journals to change its editorial tone dramatically during the decade. These popular arbiters of fashion realized that if they did not fall in line with the prevailing spirit of "anything goes" and instead continued to dictate to women what was "in" and "out", they would risk being dismissed as "fashion fascists". As a result, fashion journalists quickly adopted a new language of "freedom" and "choice".[12] The notion of anti-fashion is, therefore, not one that can be expressed solely through the wearing of shocking or oppositional fashion; as witnessed in the Seventies, it could also very much mean wearing what you felt like instead of blindly following the dictates of Paris.

This glorification of freedom in dress and personal style led the American author and journalist Tom Wolfe to dub the era the "Me Decade". Practically speaking, this meant that choosing to follow a particular fashion (let's be realistic; not everyone was able, let alone wanted, to come up with a wholly personal and individual sense of style) did not mean being willing to accept diktats. This is the reason that fashion journalists changed their tune and advertisers shifted their focus away from the brand and onto the customer by using keywords such as "freedom" and "you". Some have argued that this Me focus was a result of the hippie movement of the previous decade: with their own anti-fashions (homemade, craft, second-hand and "ethnic" dress), hippies had popularized the idea that one did not, and should not, go along with a capitalist fashion system, but should instead wear whatever one pleased. Ironically, this rejection led to a highly recognizable look that was adopted and heavily exploited by ready-to-wear companies and even Haute Couture in the 1970s.

This anti-fashion spirit combined with the Me ethos goes a long way to explain why exactly there were so many different looks. As Jacqueline Herald points out, "The problem was (that) there were lots of Me's fighting for a piece of the action."[13] It seems that the inevitable downside of freedom and choice was that many people, often in retrospect, would see this cornucopia of styles as a sign of confusion and a lack of direction. Even people at the time were confused, as borne out by Georgina Howell, who wrote in the chapter "The Uncertain Seventies" of her book *In Vogue*: "Because people disagreed about where fashion should go, it was

Oppposite
Patio dress with daisy-patterned cotton lace and integral
bib by Paco Rabanne, 1972

pulled in radically different directions." In 1991, when she came to revise the book, she tellingly changed the chapter's title to "The Schizophrenic Seventies".[14] Edmund White's recollection of the Seventies gives another perspective that illustrates this feeling of uncertainty: "For the longest time everyone kept saying the Seventies hadn't started yet. There was no distinctive style for the decade, no flair, no slogans. The mistake we made was that we were all looking for something as startling as The Beatles, acid, Pop Art, hippies and radical politics. What actually set in was a painful and unexpected working-out of the terms the Sixties had so blithely tossed off."[15]

Indeed, the social context of the early 1970s can be seen as a mixture of the continuation of late 1960s optimism but also the failure to consolidate the upheavals of 1968. Many see the start of the decade as inherently optimistic, but since '68 there had been signs that times were indeed "a-changing" if one only knew where to look. The Woodstock festival of 1969 is often held up as the glorious apotheosis of the Sixties' spirit, but The Rolling Stones concert held at Altamont only four months later can be seen as the disintegration of that same spirit. At this free festival Meredith Hunter, a young African-American man, was stabbed to death by a member of the Hell's Angels, who had been put in charge of security at the event. The realization that the free spirit of the Sixties came at a price had started to dawn – or, as Dave Harker put it, people understood that "something happened".[16] The radical changes ushered in by the Sixties contributed to the feeling of confusion, and their aftermath left people deflated and in search of yet more change when in fact society had to get to grips and work out those from the previous decade. This "one foot in the past and one foot in the present" sensibility, which marked the start of the Seventies, was clearly reflected in the fashions of the day. The fashion star of the 1960s, the mini skirt, slipped into the new decade with ease even though the Paris collections of January 1970 saw a considerable drop in hemlines all the way to the calves, which came as quite a shock after a decade marked by rising hemlines.

Of course, it needs remembering that the end of a calendar decade never marks the veritable "end of

an era", however convenient this would be for books such as this one; in stylistic terms this meant that just as certain late Sixties looks crept into the Seventies, several 1970s looks snuck into the early 1980s wardrobe. It needs emphasizing that looking only at fashion images (those specifically produced for or by the fashion industry) gives a warped view of reality. Even when the influential catwalks of the world decree that times and frocks have changed, it is unrealistic to think that everyone immediately disposes of all their now "out-of date" clothes and wholeheartedly adopts what the fashion glossies hail as the future. Hence we often get supposedly "out of date" fashions co-existing with "new" looks in the real world.

Another reason why the midi proposed by Paris was not immediately adopted universally is because it was met with considerable opposition, especially in America. Mini skirts had become a sign of youth and liberation to many in the Sixties and they were not about to do away with this visual marker just because Paris said "*non*". Beyond the symbolic attachment to the mini, there were also more practical reasons that may have contributed to the midi's slow uptake. In 1973, the first oil crisis of the decade started, with disastrous economic consequences. The UK was particularly badly hit, but the crisis's ensuing recession was felt across Western nations. To compound matters, 1973–74 saw a dramatic stock-market crash that would have a lasting economic impact. As the introduction of the falling hemline coincided with the run up to and beginning of the deepest economic downturn witnessed since the Great Depression of the 1930s, it is fair to assume that many consumers were unable or unwilling to invest in an entirely new wardrobe. Equally, many garment manufacturers, retailers and mail order businesses still had orders for, if not stockpiles of, mini skirts and hence they too were resistant to backing the new midi fashion.

Yet however great the initial resistance to the new style was, it did slowly gain in popularity and after a few years filtered over into the fashion mainstream. Maxi skirts and dresses, which had been adopted by hippies in the previous decade, also became part of everyday fashion. Although mini skirts were no longer the height of fashion after '73, having been replaced by

Opposite
Victorian-style cotton lawn and broderie anglaise
nightdress with matching mop cap by Laura Ashley, 1974

the midi and the maxi, this did not mean that legs were entirely obscured, as the new maxi skirts often featured decency-defying thigh-high splits. The slightly longer skirt got a boost from Yves Saint Laurent in 1971, when he presented a collection heavily inspired by 1940s fashions. Among his creations were a bright green boxy fox fur jacket with exaggerated shoulders, big turbans, platform shoes and over-the-knee skirts and dresses. The traditional couture clients were outraged, but the fashion press went wild. The collection also gave tweed and wool gabardine a new lease of life, and floral tea gowns became *de rigueur* for the first time since the Second World War. For those unable to afford these Parisian creations, second-hand shops were at the ready to provide young people with the originals on which these Couture creations were based. Indeed, young people had been second-hand clothes shopping to find an alternative to the fashion mainstream since the late 1950s, but the difference was that now the mainstream was producing copies of the originals and, as such, the past was no longer an "alternative".

The 1940s was not the only decade to make a sartorial comeback in the Seventies. Other decades were dragged out of the dressing-up closet, as it were, and given a second airing. In popular culture the film *Cabaret* (1972) glamorized Thirties decadence and within fashion the London-based label Biba was at the forefront of this look's revival. Biba copied 1930s Hollywood glamour but added a dark and mysterious twist: figure-hugging bias-cut maxi dresses in champagne pink, gold, leek green and cobalt blue were teamed with leopard-print faux-fur jackets or ostrich feather shrugs, and platform sandals in matching colours. The models looked like the sexy twin sisters of their 1930s counterparts with heavily made-up eyes and lips. Biba's revivalist character was not just limited to its clothes; the label's flagship store on Kensington High Street was housed in the famous 1930s Derry & Toms department store, which Barbara Hulanicki, the creator of Biba, had gone to great lengths to restore it to its former Art Deco glory. The building and its contents oozed with the glamour of bygone days. The Thirties revival was not limited to London nor to ready-to-wear; on the Parisian catwalks, interwar influences could also

easily be discerned in collections by the likes of Pierre Balmain, Thierry Mugler and Pierre Cardin.

The 1920s also made a serious comeback, especially after 1974, when *The Great Gatsby* hit the cinemas. The cloche hats, knitted skirt suits and chiffon afternoon dresses showcased in this film were created by the costume designer Theoni Aldredge (who won the Academy Award for best costume for the production), while the male wardrobe was memorably provided by Ralph Lauren, whose star rose significantly owing to his involvement with the production. While clearly based on Twenties fashion, the costumes actually have a distinctly Seventies feel about them, evidencing that historic film costume is as much about the present as it is about the past. In practical terms the film's popularity sparked a jazz-age trend and both catwalk and ready-to-wear collections delivered new versions of flapper garb, albeit in a contemporary colour scheme of beige, muted pink and peach.

The Twenties and Thirties revivals also sparked a renewed interest in fur. Fur had never gone out of fashion with the conservative elite, but was now enthusiastically adopted by young people. The trend for (second-hand) fur had started in the Sixties, but the return to glamorous fashions from the Golden Age of Hollywood saw it being worn in excess: wide fur collar and cuff-trimmed coats, fur stoles and capes, and big fur Cossack hats became fashionable outerwear. Others time-travelled still further back to *fin-de-siècle* London and Paris by donning romanticized bohemian dress associated with artistic and literary "aesthetic" circles through the adoption of fringed piano shawls, silk scarves, kimono- and Liberty-style dresses in rich brocades and crushed velvets. This look was particularly popular in Britain, where resistance to longer skirts had been much less felt than in America. Young London-based designers were, in fact, quick to take up the look for lower hemlines and combined it with a good dose of romance and bohemian chic.

This English predilection for fantasy fashion was possibly derived from the predominately liberal atmosphere of British art schools such as the Royal College of Art and Saint Martin's.[17] Designers such as Bill Gibb, Gina Fratini, Zandra Rhodes and Ossie

Clark dressed the celebrities of the day in long pliant fabrics such as crepe de chine, satin and silk chiffon, often featuring lyrical patterns. Clark and Rhodes were particularly known for their use of extravagant and distinctive prints. Whereas Clark used fabrics designed by his wife, Celia Birtwell, to great success, Rhodes's use of pattern relied on her extensive knowledge of historical and world textiles. Each collection she produced was based around a central ethnic theme such as "Japan and Lovely Lilies", "The Ukraine and Chevron Shawl" or "Mexico Sombrero and Fans".

A love for, and an excessive use of, pattern is another hallmark of the decade. An abundance of choice in pattern style, colour and size was available at all ends of the market. While now the Seventies is mostly remembered for its most excessive and ostentatious prints, it has to be remembered that aside from these multi-coloured flamboyant patterns, 1940s-style small floral, polka dot and striped prints were equally popular, they just don't make the same visual impact and are thus more easily forgotten. Historic prints, like historic designs, were given a contemporary twist through the manipulation of scale and the introduction of contemporary (often rather loud) colour schemes, and their stylistic influences spanned all the way from the 1880s to the 1950s. One designer who particularly favoured late-Victorian designs was Laura Ashley, who created dresses and accessories out of printed cottons that featured small 1880s calico prints. For her dress designs, the Welsh designer turned to the opening decade of the twentieth century. Her clothes had a distinctly Edwardian feel to them and her cotton dresses often featured ruffled necklines or hems, leg-of-mutton sleeves and lace inserts. These were worn with printed calico headscarves to complete the pastoral milkmaid look. Likewise, in America Ralph Lauren proposed a similar look in the second half of the decade, which was referred to as the Prairie Style. Cheaper versions of these rustic fashions could be purchased through the Sears Roebuck catalogue, which described them as reminiscent of early American settlers. The word "reminiscent" here is key. While the revivalist styles of the 1970s borrowed liberally from history they did not duplicate it verbatim, as is so often suggested.

The historic looks and garments that were referenced were much closer in design to their originals than fashion had previously witnessed, but to pass them of as mere copies would be denying them their rightful place in the history of fashion design and also their ability to have contemporary meaning. The meaning of fashion is specific to time and place, and when a certain item or style is revived it may look very similar, but it will not mean the same as its original. Equally, not only did Seventies designers take history and add a contemporary twist, through a new colour palette, the re-working of a pattern or the combining of different historic periods, but in so doing they also helped inspire the development of new fashion items. YSL's 1971 Forties collection, for example, featured wedge shoes and peep-toe sandals that echoed wartime styles, but which arguably also developed into platform shoes.

It is not with the design of such articles but the reasons for this historic dressing up that we find a truly novel idea underpinning the fashions of the decade. This adoption of historic fantasy styles hints at a combination of escapism and the feeling that a generation who had missed out on the "original" party – be it the free love of the 1960s or the decadent Chelsea Arts Club balls and literary salons of 1920s London – were now trying to recreate it. Through this mining of history we can discern a desire to recapture a form of authenticity, and specifically the authenticity of the past. During the Sixties, the past had been admonished in the pursuit of the forward-looking Space Age, but now futurism was itself seen as rather passé. An acknowledgement that the past was authentic implied that the present was not, and for the Seventies generation this stance made complete sense. In the face of economic hardship, they were the first generation to find comfort and safety in the past, regardless of how constructed and romanticized their idea of the past was. This borrowing can therefore be seen as a potent form of nostalgia.

Nostalgia is the expression of the feeling that the present is imperfect, but the past was perfect. Nostalgia thus invokes a positively evaluated past world in response to a defiant present world.[18] It is a way of responding to a lack in the present, and there were plenty of lacks in the Seventies: deepening economic troubles, rising unemployment, international conflict, terrorism, race riots…

So this borrowing from history is not about a generation unable to come up with something new; rather, it is about one that made a deliberate choice to revisit the past in an effort to find certainty and safety. One can't control the future, but one can certainly reshape the past to satisfy contemporary desires for stability. Neither was this simply about copying the past, as previously stated, for most designers gave their historic pastiches a contemporary twist by either using new materials and colour palettes or presenting an imagined eclectic version of history that combined different fashion elements from different periods.

This is where we have to separate nostalgia into two strands: retro nostalgia and insular nostalgia. The former takes its cue from history but infuses it with irony and hence subverts its reference. For example, Yves Saint Laurent's adaptation of wartime fashions, which attracted criticisms of "vulgarity", "kitsch" and "in bad taste", took history and played with it. This retro nostalgia grew out of the pillaging by the Sixties youth of second-hand stores and looks to create something new out of the old. These young people never set out to merely copy the past but instead used its material artefacts to create novelty by putting together pieces from different times and places. This stylistic bricolage was laden with irony and intended to be tongue-in-cheek, just as YSL's collection was meant to shock and subvert the past by addressing a problematic period in France's fashion history.

Insular nostalgia, on the other hand, presented a pastiche of the past that lacked all irony and humour. Instead of questioning history, it copied the past and made it better. Laura Ashley's Edwardian peasant dresses are the perfect example. Such garments referenced a time that was marked by rural poverty but, instead of confronting history, presented a romanticized and, more importantly, sanitized version of the period and glossed over anything problematic. Whereas retro operates on a clear value system that ascribes values to the intrinsic nature of the object, this kind of insular nostalgia "trades" in the image of the object, or

more precisely the image of a combination of objects, forming them into a coherent picture. Retro's taxonomy of material culture allows it to consider the past with unsentimental nostalgia.[19] Insular nostalgia operates as its opposite: it is loaded with sentimental and emotive nostalgia, which aligns it with kitsch, whereas retro is resolutely camp because the latter is characterized by an acknowledgement of its own ironic stance.[20] Insular nostalgia lacks self-reflection and therefore irony; it is about surface and artificial emotions and rose-tinted nostalgia for a time and place one never knew – and, even worse, for a time and place that does not and never did exist. Retro fetishizes the original whereas insular nostalgia trades on the prettified copy, the copy that bears little actual relation to the original.

Even though both forms of nostalgia are radically different in their treatment of the past, both evidence a need for stability and certainty. In times of prosperity our view is optimistic, which in fashion translates as an engagement with the future. This explains why Space Age styles by Paco Rabanne and Pierre Cardin were so influential in the Sixties. In times of crisis, however, particularly times of economic and political crisis, the present, let alone the future, is a dystopian place out of our control, whereas the past is something we can shape to satisfy contemporary needs. Equally, this disenchantment with the present and a general distrust of modern innovation were also central to this favouring of the past. It is often suggested that the fantasy fashions of the first half of the decade are a mere continuation or bubbling up of those originated with youth cultures in the Sixties, and while there is an element of truth to this, to pass them off as no more than that would be to deny the dynamic of fashion being a site where anxieties about the present are made visible.

Anxiety about the present was also expressed through another type of borrowing, not from the past but from far-flung places and cultures. Aside from times gone by, exotic cultures (exotic in this case meaning non-white, non-Western cultures) were also heavily referenced in mainstream fashion. Mexican peasant blouses and dresses, Indian scarves and Nehru jackets (a fashion mostly limited to men), colourful kaftans,

Opposite
American actress and model Anjelica Huston modelling a
multi-coloured Persian-style coat-dress with a snakeskin
belt by Bill Blass, 1970 – accessorized with Crescendoe
Superb gloves and suede boots by Herbert Levine.
Photographed by Gianni Penati

embroidered djellabahs and Eastern European folk costume became fashionable items. For those who weren't brave enough to go the whole way, elements of embroidery, fringing, smocking and crochet could add an exotic twist to more Western garments. Again these "ethnic" items had already made their debut in the hippy wardrobe but now enjoyed mainstream popularity.

This vogue for the exotic can partly be explained through the availability of cheaper air travel ensuing from the introduction of Boeing's 747 "Jumbo" jets in 1970 and the increasing uptake and affordability of package holidays. However, this cultural referencing is equally a form of nostalgia. In the same way that the past was romanticized, so were foreign cultures.

Most fashion books refer to these fashions as "ethnic", but this term is highly problematic. Rightfully they should be called "Oriental", in line with academic discourse on what constitutes the notion of "Other". The renowned literary professor Edward Said defined "Orientalism" as the Western belief that "there are Westerners, and there are Orientals. The former dominate; the latter must be dominated."[21] The Orient he speaks of is not a geographic location but rather a mental geography imposed by the West, which included Asia, Africa and South America – in essence non-white, non-Western territories and cultures. Applying this perspective to these exotic fashions complicates matters. On the one hand, the popularity of these exotic fashions and details points towards an understanding that contemporary Western fashion was merely about mass-production, financial gain and an expression of Capitalism. Yet on the other hand, it also exposed the inherent belief that these countries whose visual lexicon was referenced if not copied, albeit with alterations to suit Western needs and fashion, were somehow more authentic than the West. Whilst this can be seen as a complimentary attitude, it also reveals a deep-rooted attitude of the developed versus the underdeveloped, of the Modern West versus the pre-Modern Orient.

This isn't to say that there wasn't a genuine interest in other cultures and societies. In fact an interest in alternative, often non-Western, lifestyles had been growing since the previous decade, but it fully entered mainstream discourse in the Seventies, fuelled by the

oil crisis. Whereas in the Sixties the need for a New Direction and a back-to-the earth spirit had come from left-wing politics and hippy counter-culture, the Seventies forced the mainstream to reconsider its wasteful ways, in particular with regards to energy consumption. During this period, eco-politics gained considerable ground, as witnessed in America with the staging of the environmental movement's first Earth Day in 1970. In Britain, the same year, the BBC's television series "Doomwatch" covered a plethora of impending natural disasters and focused people's attention on what might be the long-term effects of industrialization. For many, Modernity had not only failed the economy, it was also failing "spaceship Earth".

This engagement with planet Earth and eco-politics found expression through dress with the revival of craft techniques. Again a return to the past, but in this instance it was evidenced through method rather than style. Instead of being merely nostalgic about age-old craft techniques, the handmade was seen as a worthy alternative to mass-production. Both in the UK and America, national and federal councils were set up to promote traditional crafts. Stylistically this translated into the appearance of patchwork, appliquéd, hand-knitted and crocheted garments that were either homemade or more often purchased as ready-to-wear. These craft techniques even made it into some couture collections. Again, Yves Saint Laurent had his finger on the pulse when he showed patchwork dresses and gypsy skirts on the Parisian catwalk, which the more traditional fashion press sarcastically termed as the "rich peasant" look. Regardless of such criticism, his seal of approval helped fuel the popularity of "ethnic" and craft fashions, which subsequently became available at all price points.

While this historic and cultural borrowing created some spectacular fashions, the most influential sartorial borrowing took place in a less extraordinary locale. The adoption of men's tailoring into female fashion was to have a far greater and more lasting impact than any of the themes previously mentioned. This gender borrowing happened in different ways but arguably for similar reasons: a greater sense of gender equality and a resulting need and desire for comfort. While many

Above
Laced pimento-red suede ankle-length
jumper dress worn over cable-knit jumper
and accessorized with knitted pull-on hat
and suede boots by the Israeli fashion
designer Finy Leitersdorf (left) and navy
pigskin pea coat worn over bone-coloured
suede trousers by the Israeli fashion
house Beged Or (right), 1973

hallmarks of Seventies fashion can be interpreted as conveying the erosion of strict gender divisions, the most potent has to be the mass adoption of trousers by women.

The Seventies was the era of the women's liberation movement. Following the victory in most Western nations of a woman's right to her own body with the legalization of the contraceptive pill in the 1960s, the focus now shifted to equality of opportunity in employment. The political advances women made within the workplace not only brought women greater rights and privileges but also made them acutely aware of the sartorial gender division. As increasing numbers of women on both sides of the Atlantic worked outside the home, a more practical yet stylish style of dress was needed. That said, women's entry into executive roles was not without its sartorial problems. As there was a virtually total lack of precedence in terms of women's workwear (beyond what had been adopted for lower-status jobs), women searched for more classic looks to reflect their new empowering positions. The tailored trouser and the trouser suit was a response to this need and search. Popularized in the early Seventies, trouser suits appeared in numerous guises for both day and evening wear throughout the decade. Wide flares and tailored jackets (often belted) were typical of early Seventies suits, but from the mid-decade onwards less structured jackets became dominant owing to Giorgio Armani's introduction of this looser style of garment.

As increasing numbers of women entered the higher echelons of the workforce throughout the decade, for both political and practical reasons they chose to adopt trousers, which as Valerie Steele has noted was "a development that really does seem to have reflected women's social and economic liberation".[22] This trouser suit look was soon termed the "Dress for Success Look", named after the influential dress manual by John T. Molloy, published in 1975. In 1977, the sequel, *The Women's Dress for Success Book*, was not only full of hints on how to look feminine yet authoritative in the boardroom, but more importantly it reflected just how much gender-defying sartorial progress had been made in the decade. Another outcome of feminist politics was the abandonment of the fun, little-girl look that

had characterized Sixties dolly-bird fashions. Instead, women preferred to look like adults as they realized that if they were to claim their rightful place as men's equals in the workplace they had to dress as their equals. That isn't to say that women slavishly copied the male wardrobe and rejected femininity per se (this only happened in the extreme corners of radical feminism), but certainly a more serious businesslike look, especially within the realm of workwear, was explored.

This search for a more mature and sober look was also reflected in a shift, or a widening, of popular hair and make-up styles. As with fashion, the Seventies evidenced a wide range of fashionable hairstyles and make-up trends. Hair was initially mostly worn long and straight in either a middle or side parting. Soon a vogue for waved and demi-curled hair appeared, which reached the height of its popularity after 1976 owing to Farah Fawcett's iconic appearance in the hit TV series "Charlie's Angels". This curled hairdo came as a godsend to those with naturally frizzy hair and offered women an escape from the long straight hair look, which had distinctly innocent-little-girl connotations. Disco fever would see hair grow to bigger proportions still through waving, perming and crimping. The influence of race politics could also be discerned through hair and beauty culture: not only were black models featured for the first time in fashion and beauty imagery created for a white market, several proudly donned the Afro instead of falling in line with a homogenous Western ideal of straightened hair; certain white men and women adopted the Afro with varying degrees of success. The influence of black beauty culture was also evinced in 1979, when the actress Bo Derek famously sported blonde braided cornrows in the film *Ten.*

Like hair, make-up was also a matter of personal choice. Those adopting the "Dress for Success" look often favoured a nude (i.e. minimal) make-up look to reinforce their desire to be taken seriously by shaking off the most obvious trappings of femininity, while other women indulged in all that face paint had to offer. Lipstick was popular throughout the decade, but the first half of the decade favoured more muted natural tones, whereas the latter part saw a vogue for

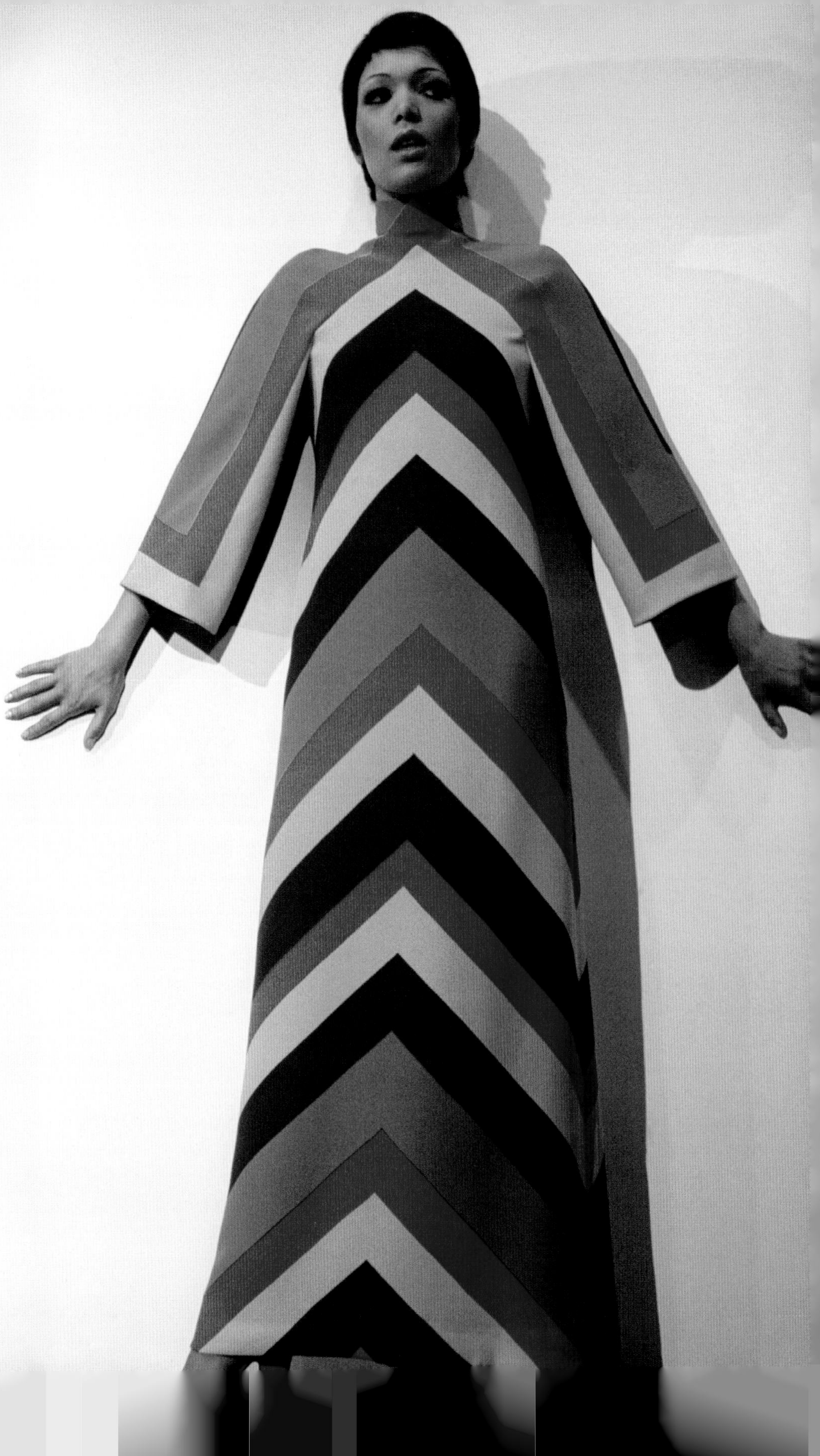

increasingly bright red lips. This again seems to fall in line with the abandonment of the little-girl look, which had favoured the accentuation of the eyes through fake lashes, eyeliner or eye shadow to create big Bambi peepers, and the shift to a more mature womanly look; even the most conservative and androgynous trouser or skirt suit could be turned into a sexier evening look through the application of some bright red lipstick.

Aside from the trouser suit, skirt suits often in serious "masculine" materials such as tweed were equally popular as they featured a more androgynous top half but a feminine bottom half. Interestingly, knitted skirt suits also made a return to the fashion stage, having been introduced in the 1920s by Coco Chanel and Jean Patou. In that period, which had also witnessed a seismic advancement in women's rights, they had been hailed as the ideal outfit for working women, so their reappearance in the 1970s was very fitting and again a clear indication that revivalist styles were far from random, empty or mere superficial copies of the past.

Jeans performed a similar role in daywear to that of the tailored trousers at the office. According to Elizabeth Ewing, jeans became a mode of dress that was "irrespective of sex"[23] and gained widespread popularity and acceptance during the Seventies after decades of being seen as workwear, and then as a symbol of youth and counterculture during the Sixties. The jeans-and-a-T-shirt look became an almost unofficial unisex uniform for both men and women during the decade.[24] As Steele notes, "Yet even as jeans became 'co-opted' by the fashion system, their signifying value grew more powerful. But popular awareness of different brands and styles subverted the old utopian idea that everyone would be equal in identical jeans. Levi's and Wrangler had to compete with a host of new 'designer' blue jeans, produced by companies like Fiorucci, Gloria Vanderbilt, Pierre Cardin and Calvin Klein."[25]

Jeans, like other trousers, came in a variety of styles, but flared legs were by far the most popular and distinctive look of the Seventies, with trendy "baggy" jeans being popularized by Elio Fiorucci only in the late Seventies. Flares themselves could range from a modest boot flare to an exaggerated full-leg flare, and trousers could be plain or printed in wild patterns; checked and pinstripe fabrics were also hugely popular. Velvets and corduroys in practically every colour of the rainbow were also used, but the former was particularly popular for the short-lived fashion oddity: hot pants. These clingy, butt-hugging micro shorts enjoyed a brief spell of popularity, albeit mostly only with the very young, at the start of the decade, and while they might seem outrageous to modern eyes, they were worn both for leisure and at work. Rather than being considered offensive, hot pants were essentially the trouser counterpart of the mini skirt and as such were simply viewed as a fun item that signalled a free and liberated attitude.

So whereas the first half of the Seventies was dominated by frequently outrageous fantasy, retro, pastiche and "ethnic" styles with an orientation towards youth, freedom of choice and the countercultural values associated with anti-capitalism and eco-politics, things would change dramatically in the second half of the decade. From around 1975 through to late 1979, fashions became both more conservative and severe. In youth and street fashions, the designer hippy ethos of freedom and choice was followed by the nihilistic and shocking styles of punk. Similarly, on the catwalks the earlier ostentatious and excessive fashions were replaced by a stricter yet no less shocking style that is now commonly referred to as "Terrorist Chic". The middle classes, meanwhile, increasingly gravitated towards the uniformity of the "Dress for Success" look, signalling the advent of the dominant power-dressing look of the 1980s.

This shift in youth culture towards the violence and deliberate bad taste of punk fashions and the middle classes' increasingly conservative look was born out of the same reasons: the deepening economic crisis, political upheaval and social fragmentation. But where the former chose to confront these social ills, the latter tried to adjust to them and fit in through the adoption of a uniform style.

Born in London in 1976 – although arguably there was also a localization of American punk stage acts such as the New York Dolls and the Ramones – the punk movement was predominantly made up of

Above
Italian fashion designer and entrepreneur Elio Fiorucci
posing with his sales assistants in his Milan store, 1974

unemployed youth, a group that had grown to worryingly high proportions, and disaffected art students. Punk promoted anarchy, nihilism and an outright rejection of middle-class notions of good taste. In opposition to the hippy youth culture style, its clothes were generally black and deliberately menacing. Punks, like hippies before them, adopted a do-it-yourself ethos and either made their own clothes or customized second-hand garments. For those with more money to burn, Vivienne Westwood and Malcolm McLaren's Seditionaries boutique and the Great Gear Market – both on the King's Road in Chelsea – sold bondage trousers, T-shirts with sexually/politically explicit or obscene statements or imagery, and "ugly" mohair jumpers in garish colours. In addition to these staples, the punk style lexicon included leather jackets embellished with studs, chains and/or customized with painted slogans, skin-tight black trousers, various items of fetish and bondage wear, Dr Martens boots and crepe-soled brothel creepers.

Female punks could also add plastic, rubber, PVC or animal print miniskirts, fishnet or holed tights, and menacingly sharp stiletto heels. Garments for both sexes were adorned with safety pins, studs, chains, zippers and even razor blades. Hair and make-up played as important a role in punk as did clothes. Both sexes' hair was dyed either jet black or in bright colours, and was often shaved at the sides and gelled up to create the Mohican, a style taken from Mohawk Indians. Female punks also frequently sported closely cropped masculine-looking hairstyles or razor-cut spikes. Make-up was not used to beautify but rather to create a shocking appearance. Eyes were heavily made up in dark or garish colours, while lips and nails were painted black – punk intentionally created an anti-aesthetic and in this sense can be seen, particularly for women, to have been a liberating force.

These extreme looks were very much limited to disenchanted and disenfranchised youth and were impossible for the fashion industry to adopt or co-opt because they were in direct opposition to all it stood for. Nevertheless, as the decade progressed, aspects of the style began to bubble up, mostly through the medium of female music stars such as Debbie Harry, Poly

Styrene and Siouxsie Sioux. Obviously, such borrowings were highly sanitized, and commercialized by both the mass market and high fashion brands. In 1977, Zandra Rhodes's collection featured slashed jersey dresses festooned with safety pins, but aside from a few less aggressive elements making it into the mainstream, punk's influence and indeed its legacy lay in the fact that it firmly re-established London as the capital of subculture and youth innovation.

While punk style and music was essentially nihilistic, Glam presented a far more upbeat image, though arguably its over-the-top excess, gender-bending and spectacular nature can be seen as an escapist reaction to the societal ills that punk chose to confront head-on. While Glam artists, like punk and funk artists, were very popular, it would be wrong to assume that what they wore on stage was fashion. These acts were primarily centred on "performance" and thus their costumes were never intended to be Fashion. This does not mean they did not influence mainstream styles, for like with punk, watered-down and more wearable versions of their costumes did cross over into the mainstream, but their role in shaping mainstream fashion should not be exaggerated either. The most recognizable of these "cross-over" items were platform shoes and boots worn by acts as diverse as David Bowie, Isaac Hayes and George Clinton, which were available in a wide variety of colours, designs and materials and became fashion items for both men and women. Music genres and stars thus clearly impacted on fashion, but to varying degrees.

Arguably the most successful music look to filter through to mainstream fashion was put forward by Disco acts. Although Disco's roots pre-date the Seventies, it was in around 1974 that it surged in popularity, with the craze culminating in 1977 with the film *Saturday Night Fever*. Disco fashions had their origin in dance wear and therefore leotards, body stockings and shorts were all essential elements of the look, as were flowing and draped mini and maxi dresses, which had a distinctive Grecian feel about them and which allowed free movement of the body. Those who went out disco dancing also favoured Lycra and other stretchy fabrics that allowed the body to move unhindered, and fashion designers were

quick to latch on to this look. The American designer
Halston was particularly influential in this regard. He
created soft, often draped, relatively unconstructed,
separates perfect for dancing. For his creations he
favoured the artificial fibre Ultrasuede and the silky
knit fabric known as "liquid jersey". His fluid halter-neck
jumpsuits, blouses, dresses and trousers were worn by
the celebrities of the day in the ultra trendy epicenter
of disco: Studio 54. As *Women's Wear Daily* gushed:
"The 1970s belong to Halston."

These disco styles also impacted significantly on
leisurewear, which took on board the comfortable
and sporty elements of the look and combined them
with classic elements to provide people with casual
yet fashionable separates. Aside from this casual
leisurewear that emerged from America, the late
Seventies saw two discernable styles emerge in the
field of high fashion: Terrorist Chic and the fashion for
looser and far less structured garments.

While punk with its extreme styles had made
relatively little impact on mainstream fashions, it had
picked up on and translated the sinister growing
undercurrent of (sexual) violence and brutality. As
Steele points out, "1970s fashion, in general, was heavily
influenced by what one American scholar [Michael
Selzer] described as 'Terrorist Chic'. Black leather
became stylish, precisely because it evoked images
of sado-masochistic sex, which was regarded as 'the
last taboo'." Pornographic movies like *Angelique in
Black Leather* and the homoerotic *Nights in Black
Leather* contributed to the mystique, as did art films like
Maitresse, which was about a dominatrix, and featured
fetish costumes in leather and rubber by Karl Lagerfeld.
Even department store windows featured mannequins
that were blindfolded, tied up and shot. Fashion
photography, in particular, was implicated in the new
style,[26] through photographers such as Helmut Newton
and Guy Bourdin; the former featured women in highly
charged sexual situations and outfits, while the latter
demonstrated a penchant for brutalized or seemingly
dead female bodies.

Aside from these fetish-inspired fashions and
fashionable representations, this brutality came to the
fore in the late 1970s collections of Daniel Hechter, who
dressed women in tweed suits teamed with black berets
and leather coats, which appeared to reference the
IRA. Developing alongside this rather shocking brutal
style was the looser, yet often more conservative, trend,
which was both a continuation and diversification of
the "Dress for Success" look that had emerged earlier
in the decade. In particular, Japanese designers such
as Issey Miyake started showing layered and wrapped
silhouettes, which favoured unstructured separates yet
remained appropriate work wear. These wrap fashions
tended to cover rather than expose the body and did
not accentuate the erogenous zones, which is why they
can be seen as more conservative in comparison to
the decade's other looks. The use of textured knitwear
became popular as a result of this less-structured trend
because it added a modicum of shape to a relaxed
garment and allowed for the introduction of pattern in a
far less overt way than had been witnessed at the start
of the decade.

The Seventies closed as it had opened with a variety
of styles and looks that all fell under the banner of
Fashion; no single look came out victorious as being
definitive of the era. The suit in all its different guises
was, however, the only fashion to have lasted the
course of the decade and would, of course, take centre
stage in the next as a symbol of women who wanted
to get and were getting ahead. However, instead of
disregarding the decade because it did not present one
coherent style, the Seventies should be celebrated for
its fragmentation: not only did it popularize the notion of
personal freedom and style over the elitist rule of Paris,
it also paved the way for our contemporary shopping
landscape of choice. What *Vogue* had predicted in
1970 has to a large extent been realized thanks to
the Seventies: "Clothes (…) are purely for decoration
and they have more to do with you in particular than
anything in general."

Footnotes

1. Christopher Booker, *The Seventies: Portrait of a Decade*, (Penguin Books, 1980), p.4

2. This is far from the first time that 1970s looks have made it back onto the catwalk and into the wardrobes of the fashion conscious. In fact, as early as the 1980s certain elements of popular dress of the previous decade were already making a re-appearance on the fashion stage.

3. Leon Hunt, *British Low Culture: From Safari Suits to Sexploitation,* (Routledge, 2013), p.67

4. Daniel Roche, *A History of Everyday Things*, (Cambridge University Press, 2000), p.193

5. Ted Polhemus, *Street Style*, (Pymca, 2010)

6. Valerie Steele, "Anti-Fashion: The 1970s", *Fashion Theory: The Journal of Dress, Body & Culture*, Volume 1, Number 3, (Berg Journals/Bloomsbury Journals, 1997)

7. The deliberate use of the capital "F" is to separate fashionable styles from high Fashion created or, better put, dictated by the Haute Couture salons of Paris, whose silhouettes ordinarily filtered down through cheap copies into the wardrobes of women worldwide.

8. Valerie Steele, "Anti-Fashion: The 1970s", *Fashion Theory: The Journal of Dress, Body & Culture*, Volume 1, Number 3, (Berg Journals/Bloomsbury Journals, 1997)

9. Elizabeth Ewing, *History of 20th Century Fashion*, (Batsford, 2001), p.232

10. Jacqueline Herald, *Fashions of a Decade,* (Chelsea House Publishers, 2007), p.24

11. Nicola White & Ian Griffiths, *The Fashion Business: Theory, Practice, Image*, (Berg, 2000), p.13

12. Valerie Steele, "Anti-Fashion: The 1970s", *Fashion Theory: The Journal of Dress, Body & Culture,* Volume 1, Number 3, (Berg Journals/Bloomsbury Journals, 1997), p. 280

13. Jacqueline Herald, *Fashions of a Decade: The 1970s*, (Chelsea House Publishers, 2007)

14. Valerie Steele, Anti-Fashion: The 1970s, *Fashion Theory: The Journal of Dress, Body & Culture*, Volume 1, Number 3, (Berg Journals/Bloomsbury Journals, 1997), p.280

15. Valerie Steele, Anti-Fashion: The 1970s, *Fashion Theory: The Journal of Dress, Body & Culture*, Volume 1, Number 3, (Berg Journals/Bloomsbury Journals, 1997), p.79

16. Dave Harker, *One for the Money: Politics and Popular Song*, (Hutchinson, 1980), p.103

17. See: Valerie D. Mendes & Amy De La Haye, *20th Century Fashion*, (Thames & Hudson, 1999)

18. Stuart Tannock, "Nostalgia Critique" in *Cultural Studies*, 9 (3), (Routledge, 1995), p.454

19. Elizabeth E. Guffey, *Retro, The Culture of Revival*, (Reaktion Books, 2006)

20. Susan Sontag, "Notes on Camp", *Against Interpretation and Other Essays*, (Penguin Books, 2009)

21. Edward W. Said, *Orientalism*, (Vintage Books/Random House, 1978), p.36

22. Valerie Steele, "Anti-Fashion: The 1970s", Fashion Theory: *Fashion Theory: The Journal of Dress, Body & Culture*, Number 3, (Berg Journals/Bloomsbury Journals, 1997), p.284

23. Elizabeth Ewing, *History of 20th Century Fashion*, (Batsford, 2001), p.238

24. Elizabeth Ewing, *History of 20th Century Fashion*, (Batsford, 2001), p.238

25. Valerie Steele, "Anti-Fashion: The 1970s", *Fashion Theory: The Journal of Dress, Body & Culture*, Volume 1, Number 3, (Berg Journals/Bloomsbury Journals, 1997), p.285

26. "Anti-Fashion: The 1970s", *Fashion Theory: The Journal of Dress, Body & Culture*, Volume 1, Number 3, (Berg Journals/Bloomsbury Journals, 1997), p.289

1970s Daywear

The Seventies witnessed a huge variety of fashionable daywear looks to choose from. While some silhouettes and items, such as the suit, remained popular throughout the decade, the majority had a far shorter lifespan. Some, like hot pants, only lasted just over a year. It is always difficult to pinpoint the exact moment something goes from being in fashion to out of fashion. Fashion magazines are a great source to discover where designers and fashion editors think fashion is going, but one can't rely on them to give an accurate representation of what people are actually wearing. While designers may decree a fashion is over by radically changing the silhouette or by adding or doing away with certain garments or styles from their collections, this does not mean that the buying public follow suit. Initially there is often resistance to radically new fashions, and while in the end the majority of styles do manage to filter through, this process can take a fair while. Hence we often see many different looks happily co-existing.

This was indeed the case in the Seventies, but the reason why there were so many different, and at times radically different, styles around was rooted in much more than the mere cycle of fashion. The prevailing ethos of the era was one of individualism. Hence it was first decade that put personal style and taste above fashion and that encouraged people to do their own thing rather than sheepishly follow the dictates of designers. So not only did many looks co-exist at any given time, they were all "in" fashion, as fashion itself was redefined along very different, more personal lines. It is impossible to catalogue the entirety of this plethora of daywear styles, but it is possible to pick up on some tendencies that made their mark on the decade. The most important one is comfort; whatever style women chose to adopt, from the mini skirt to the jumpsuit or the trouser suit to the maxi dress, all styles had an inherent element of comfort to them, representing in clothing the advances of the women's movement.

While some Seventies daywear fashions to the contemporary eye might seem silly, childish or highly sexualized, they need to be contextualized correctly. The cute mini dresses and baby-dolls in fun bright colours and prints were often a symbol of liberation and freedom of choice in the Seventies, not necessarily of sexualization. It is vitally important to remember that those who wore these fun childlike fashions chose to do so. They were under no obligation nor pressure to wear these items. For the first time, women had fashionable alternatives in the mainstream and they could pick and choose the look they felt like; some chose pretty and girly, while others chose elegantly ladylike, some opted for soberly conservative, while others preferred a more bold and in-your-face statement. This spirit of individuality, freedom and fun is reflected in many daywear styles, through their bright colour palette, the odd dimensions of clothes (either very big or very small) and the liberal use of pattern. For those less keen on these cute and fun styles (radical feminism in particular took offence at these girl-women, but it is fair to say that during the Seventies radical feminism was generally anti-fashion), there were many alternatives. Working women favoured trousers, trouser suits and skirt suits, but even within these items there was huge variety. Trousers could be bought in conservative tweeds of muted tones, in wild colourful prints and pretty much anything in between. Arguably jeans were the most popular type of trouser, and during the Seventies they shook off their countercultural identity and were co-opted into the fashionable daywear wardrobe. Ever versatile, jeans could be dressed up with a blouse for the office or teamed with a T-shirt for more relaxed occasions.

In the workplace, however, more traditional materials and male tailoring were generally favoured. This borrowing of male tailoring is again a clear reflection of the breakdown of traditional gender barriers that was taking place right throughout the decade. Skirt suits were another more mature alternative and again came in a variety of styles and fabrics but enjoyed particular popularity in knitted fabrics – another clear indicator of the modern woman's need for comfort. These knitted ensembles were very reminiscent of those popularized in the 1920s by Coco Chanel and Jean Patou, and were often accessorized in a similar manner with cloche hats or berets. This 1920s revivalist look was

far from the only historic style to be popularized in the decade; other historic eras were equally mined for their sartorial potential. The streets were filled with Edwardian milkmaids, 1940s gauche gamines, Twenties flappers and *fin-de-siècle* Bohos. Aside from history fashion, designers also borrowed heavily from non-Western cultures, especially in regards to pattern, although some "ethnic" items such as the kaftan did find their way into the fashionable wardrobe.

Traditional craft techniques were also revived as part of this sartorial return to the past; patchwork, appliqué, crochet and textured knitwear were incorporated into both ready-to-wear and high fashion. Skirts of all lengths were fashionable, particularly in the first half of the decade when women could choose to show off or obscure their legs by donning either the mini or the maxi, and for those who wanted a bit of both, the midi was the perfect answer. The second half of the decade favoured the over-the-knee skirt, but even then the very young did not abandon the mini altogether. The closing years of the decade in fact saw a new incarnation of the mini, albeit in a less cute and innocent guise than before. Punks wore minis made out of leather, PVC, rubber and plastic to deliberately shock and provoke. Punk style had minimal impact on mainstream fashion but was one of the contributing factors to the growing fashion for black clothes that started toward the end of the Seventies and that would go on to dominate the Eighties.

Opposite
Loulou de la Falaise,
English-born model,
fashion muse and style
icon, wearing a peasant-
style dress, 1970 –
photographed by Bert Stern

Above
American actress Natalie Wood
modelling a hand-printed chrome-yellow
felt long dress adorned with a swirling
scarlet pattern by Zandra Rhodes and
accessorized with rings by Cadoro, c.1970
– photographed by Gianni Penati

Above
British model Caroline Coon wearing an embroidered satin and polyester mask-motif "Tongue" dress by the Japanese designer Kansai Yamamoto, 1971 – Yamamoto held his first London fashion show in 1971 and around this time his fashion empire boasted an impressive annual turnover of £1,000,000

Opposite
Models wearing vibrantly coloured short-suits with bold Japanese motifs and platform boots by Japanese designer Kansai Yamamoto, 1971 – the model on the right is Marie Helvin, who was famously married to the fashion photographer David Bailey

Left
Cap-sleeved floral patterned
smock worn over pastel
knit dress by Paul Maris,
1972 – according to the
San Francisco Examiner,
this design was "a whimsical
adaption of baseball uniform"

Opposite
Striped and floral patterned silk
knit long skirt with matching
dolman-sleeve wrap top, 1972

Daywear

Right
"Miss Paris" (Pascale Egurbide)
modelling the "Pivoine" summer
ensemble in white and multicoloured
fabric designed by the Parisian tailor
Hyacinthe Novak, 1973

Opposite
Dee Caperton, a former "Miss West
Virginia", modelling peach and
mahogany-brown "Parquet" wide-
leg high-rise trousers in suede and
carpet-weave cloth by Mountain
Artisan, 1972

Above
Model poses in a brown mini dress
with bib neckline, Britain, c.1970 –
photographed by Jamie Hodgson

Above
Model poses in a magenta mini shirtdress
worn with a gold chain belt, Britain, c.1970 –
photographed by Jamie Hodgson

Opposite
Tailored pant suit with trapunto stitched jacket by
Givenchy (right) and similarly tailored pant suit
made using Vogue 2920 pattern and executed
in Dacron polyester (left) – the latter costing
$43.50 to make, 1974

Above
Crocheted black-and-white harlequin
pants with matching silk shirt and knitted
black smock jacket by Adolfo, 1972

Above
Five models posing on Les Champs-Elysées
wearing garments from Jean Rychter's 1974
Spring/Summer collection, 1973

Opposite
"Four Seasons" fashion collection by Parisian
couturier Jean Barthet for Kores International,
a well-known manufacturer of office accessories
– with the four ensembles made from carbon
paper, machine ribbon, metallic film and stencils
produced by Kores, 1974

Daywear

Opposite
Fringed white-matte jersey dancing dress by
Adèle Simpson, 1974 – showing the influence
of 1920s fashions with its accentuated hip line

Below
"Foxtrot" jersey ballet-style dress with ballooning
sleeves by Jean Varon & Capricorne, 1972

Above
Navy, red and orange knit dress with white collar – which was described by a fashion consultant as having "executive appeal" in the *San Francisco Examiner* – and a green satin shirt worn with a plaid woollen skirt and green suede jacket by Anne Klein that was seen as suitable for the "board room", 1973

Opposite
Mini dress with a bib and voluminous shoulders worn over a jumper by Prêt-à-Porter, 1972

REALISATION
Jacque Lamarche
"Léo"
Mont Royal Peint.
assurance Bélair

Right
Pale green woollen lace
polo dress with knitted
collar, cuffs and hem-band
worn with matching woollen
hat and X-strap leather
shoes by Pierre Cardin for
his 1975/1976 Autumn/
Winter Collection

Opposite
Multicoloured zip-fronted
knitted coat-dress and
matching hat by the
Montreal fashion designer
Francine Vandelac, 1973

Above left
Burgundy cobra skin suit with fur collar
and cuffs worn with matching hat, 1973

Above right
Evening suit with fox collar by the Rome-
based designer Beatrice di Borbone,
1972

Opposite
Knitted and crocheted multi-toned suits
trimmed with fur by Adolfo, 1972

Daywear

Above
Three flower-print silk crepe
ensembles worn with crocheted
headbands by Pierre Balmain, 1975

Above
Peasant-style printed silk quilted
jacket worn with printed silk turban,
frilled taffeta skirt and sweater top by
Yves Saint Laurent, 1974

Daywear

Left
Wide pleated skirt and blouse in black, brown and beige printed crepe with matching belt knotted around waist, by Pierre Cardin, 1974

Opposite
Short-sleeved white shantung jacket worn with white and blue polka dot silk blouse and pleated printed silk skirt in marine blue, white, mid-blue and beige, and blue cotton short-sleeved jacket worn with checked silk blouse and pleated skirt in marine blue, yellow and white – both by Emanuel Ungaro, 1973

Daywear

Above
Velour jersey jacket worn with fine jersey
blue-and-white patterned skirt and
striped pullover by Rodier, 1974

Above
Jumper and skirt ensemble made from
Gwendacril jacquard (plum and mauve
on blue) from the "Harmoniques"
collection presented by the textile
division of Rhône-Poulenc, 1972

Daywear

Above
Striped artificial silk dress with
matching scarf by English designer
David Butler, 1976

Opposite
Cotton mini dress with matching sun
hat intended for holidays and the
beach (left) and a long skirt worn with
scooped-neckline top and matching
hat (right) – both by Mary Quant, 1973

Daywear

Above
"Gentaine" botanical print silk jersey
dress and matching hat by Leonard,
1976

Opposite
Long dress and short dress in fine cotton
toile with flower pattern print worn with
straw sunhats by Jean Dieudonné, 1974

Opposite
Wool crepe dress with panelled
shoulder and waist sections by
Philippe Deville, 1977

Above
High-waist and full-skirted printed silk twill
dresses – one in red and green and the other in
blue and green – by Jacques Esterel, 1974

Above
Lilac jersey afternoon dress
with flounced skirt by Philippe
Salvert, 1977

Daywear

Dress with raised waistline over a fluted
skirt to accentuate waistline by French-
born American fashion designer Pauline
Trigère, 1972

Above left
Plaid cotton dress and short-sleeved acrylic-knitted V-necked cardigan worn with denim skirt by Frank et Fils, 1974 – both accessorized with scarves and straw hats

Above right
Soft raspberry silk shantung safari suit by Victor Joris and apricot-and-beige silk linen shirtdress by Kasper, 1973

Opposite
Checked woollen tunic-style blouse worn over matching skirt and accessorized with a thin leather belt and strings of beads, *Ligne Elegante*, Winter 1974/75

1062

Top left
Fashion sketch of a long fitted waistcoat with patterned panels worn over a blue roll-neck sweater and white flared trousers by Mortone Vogue, 1970s

Top right
Fashion sketch of a lime-green dress suit with a side-pleated skirt by Mortone Vogue, 1970s

Left
Fashion sketch of a baby-blue-and-grey checked jacket worn with a matching over-the-knee A-line skirt by Mortone Vogue, 1970s

Mortone Vogue.   MV. 4140.

Left
Fashion sketch of bibbed
dungaree-style two-tone
brown hot pants worn over a
white blouse with billowing
sleeves and accessorized
with white leather platform
boots by Mortone Vogue,
1970s

Daywear

Right
Dots and Stripes: polka-dot trouser
suit worn with a striped scarf-necked
blouse and wide buckled belt, 1972
– the beret shows the influence of
1920s fashions on designers working
in the Seventies

Opposite
Female workers at Eastman Dillon,
Union Securities & Co. in Chicago
resolving "the mini-maxi-midi
confusion" by wearing as a "one-day
experiment" pant suits while punching
in for work, 1970

Left
Dolman-sleeved dress with wide
midriff panel to accentuate waistline
by Daniel Hechter, 1973 – available as
a Butterick pattern

Opposite
Cotton T-shirt worn with cotton polka-
dot printed skirt by Prisunic, 1974

Above
Two tweed suit ensembles – one in blue and beige and the other in pink and blue – by London-based designer Hardy Amies, 1974

Opposite
Norfolk suit in brown-and-rust herringbone tweed by Ralph Lauren for Polo, 1973

Above left

Sketch of a design from Lanvin's 1972
Spring/Summer Collection showing
a Spring suit with pleated short skirt,
long belted jacket and bow-tied blouse

Above right

Sketch of a design from Lanvin's 1972 Spring/
Summer Collection showing boldly striped tunic
top worn over a slim short skirt and accessorized
with a giant white cravat and spotted hat

Above left
Sketch of a design from Louis
Feraud's 1972 Spring/Summer
Collection showing frilly cap-
sleeved dress with ruffled skirt

Above right
Sketch of a design from Louis
Feraud's 1972 Spring/Summer
Collection showing dress with
plunging neckline and short hemline

Daywear

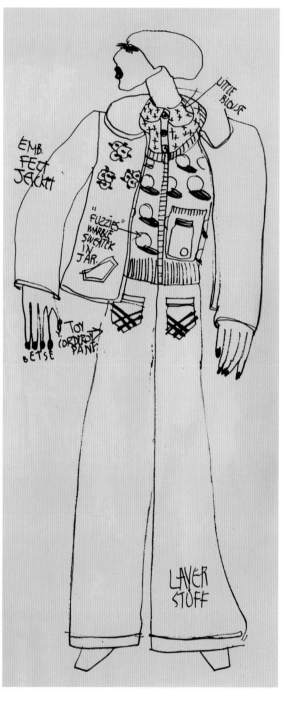

Above left
Design sketch by Betsey Jackson showing sailor top and matching trousers in shirt-cotton, 1972

Above right
Design sketch by Betsey Jackson showing a layered ensemble comprising an embroidered felt jacket, a jar-patterned knitted "shrink", a printed blouse and wide corduroy trousers

Opposite
Model wearing a green velour top with pink satin lapels and matching pink satin tight-waisted flared trousers embellished with heart-shaped patchwork motifs by Mr Freedom, 1971

Left
Grey jersey-tweed dress worn
with tight fitting knitted hat by
Rodier-Club, 1974

Opposite
Peasant-style printed wool
crepe blouse and skirt worn
with a cloth waistcoat and a
knitted woollen hat by Yves
Saint Laurent, 1976

Daywear

Above
Dolman-sleeved top and matching skirt in chevron-
and plaid-patterned knitted silk by Missoni, 1972

Opposite
Mille-fleur printed cotton top and matching
handkerchief-hemmed skirt by Gunne Saxe (left),
and chintz-printed skirt worn with V-necked blouse
(centre) and dark voile printed skirt worn with
bandeau (right) – both by The Company, 1973

Opposite
Blouson-pleated peach crepe
dress by Lew Prince for Larry
Aldrich accessorized with a
long pearl rope necklace, 1973

Above
Pleated shantung crepe dress with a
full skirt and billowing sleeves worn
with a matching fringed scarf by
Emanuel Ungaro, 1974

N°. 656
Mod. Dolce Estate

Opposite left
Illustration of "Cillia" outfit comprising
a pea-green tunic top and matching
skirt featuring buttoned detailing, worn
over a polo-collared orange blouse by
Eva, Italy, c.1973

Opposite right
Illustration of mustard-ellow "Bazar"
coat-dress with scalloped detailing and
accessorized with matching shoes, gloves
and handbag, and a wide-brimmed blue
hat by Eva, Italy, c.1973

Above
Illustration of bright orange "Dolce Estate"
mini culotte dress with V-shaped waistband
and applied pocket features worn with
contrasting green shoes and headband by
Eva, Italy, c.1973

Left
Red, black and white polka
dot knitted two-piece suit
worn with a pointed collar
striped shirt and cream
jumper by Leo Greer and
accessorized with a brown
printed velveteen hat by
Madcaps and a brown
leather and red suede
belt by Vacher, c.1971
– photographed by J.P.
Zachariasen

Opposite
Long cardigan with tailored
collar worn over a blue-and-
white striped pullover and a
soft jersey skirt by Korrigan,
1973 – accessorized with
printed silk scarf and wide-
brimmed hat

Right
Clingy tobacco and navy
dotted crepe-de-chine
dress with bow-tied neck
and worn with a matching
hat by Christian Dior, 1974

Opposite
Knitted coral jacket worn
with matching skirt and
maroon jumper by Victor
Joris for Cuddlecoat,
1970 – accessorized with
a double-buckled belt by
Etienne Aigner, a maroon
leather clutch bag by Saber
and a floppy wide-brimmed
maroon hat

Right
White cardigan worn over a navy-and-white sweater and white knit skirt from Macy's (left), denim suit worn with a orange halter from The Emporium (centre) and beige-and-black knitted top with Art Deco print skirt and matching cardigan from Joseph Magnin (right), 1973

Opposite
Green-and-white striped dress with matching short-sleeved jacket worn with a wide white belt, 1976

Right
Soft brown toned silk print
suit comprising a cardigan
jacket, a pleated skirt and
a complimentary patterned
blouse by Oscar de la Renta,
1972 – accessorized with a
fashionable beret

Orange baseball-style sweater with
navy trim and applied flower motif
worn with checked blouse and
geometric patterned skirt by Emanuel
Ungaro, 1972

Above
Printed crepe-de-chine dress
with Lurex threads and integrated
belt, and similar long dress worn
with a matching blouson jacket by
Torrente, 1972

Above
Two "Lollipop Stripe" printed
shirtdresses with "Corselet"
belts by Louis Féraud, 1972

Above
Long woollen cardigan trimmed with fox fur worn
over a silk blouse and a tweed wrap skirt for
Yves Saint Laurent's Autumn/Winter 1973/74
collection – accessorized with a felt cloche hat

Left
Grey woollen jacket worn
over matching skirt and with a
white blouse and dark pullover
by Halston, 1972 – note the
fashionable wrap chain belt with
its toothlike pendant

Right
Black-and-white checked
"Dairy Maid" dress with
lace trim and a bow belt by
London-based designer,
Jean Allen, 1972

Opposite
A presentation of French
fashion in London – here
showing a turquoise wool
dress with billowing sleeves,
large buttons and a tie belt
by Emesse, 1972

Left
Swirling-patterned dress with large pointed collar, bishop sleeves and flaring trumpet skirt, *Ligne Élégante*, Winter 1974/75

Opposite, top left
Two-tone blue patterned dress with matching back-opening fitted jacket and worn with a long grey scarf, *Ligne Élégante*, 1971

Opposite, top right
Red woollen jersey wrap dress with decorative button detailing and worn with a wide leather belt with large metal buckle, *Ligne Élégante*, Winter 1971

Opposite, bottom left
Green-and-white mini dress with matching coat and hat shown in background, *Ligne Élégante*, 1971

Opposite, bottom right
Brown dress with long white pointed collar and a double-skirted section fastened with large metal buckle, *Ligne Élégante*, 1971

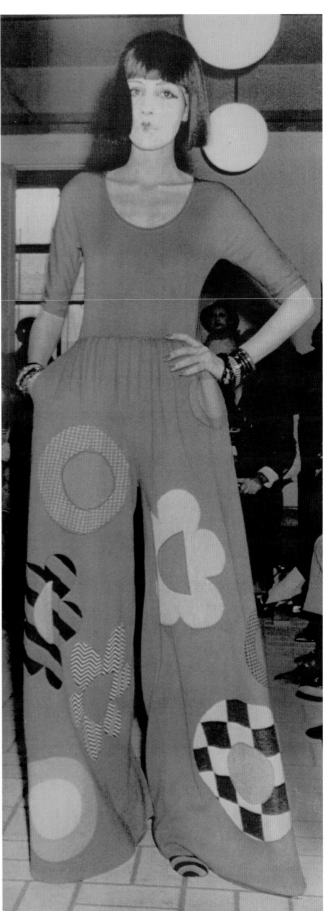

Left
Black-and-white checked,
high-necked sheath evening
dress with large pink and
orange flower motifs designed
by Rudi Gernreich as part of his
"China Flavour Look" collection
for Harmon Knitwear, 1973
– note the Oriental influence
reflected in the model's
Geisha-like white face make-
up, heavily blackened eyes,
heart-shaped mouth and black
Mandarin-bob wig

Opposite left
Culotte-playsuit with
sweetheart neckline in a bold
floral pattern overlaid with
diagonal stripes designed by
Rudi Gernreich as part of his
"China Flavor Look" collection
for Harmon Knitwear, 1973

Opposite right
Palazzo jumpsuit with bold
floral patterning and scooped
neckline designed by Rudi
Gernreich as part of his "China
Flavor Look" collection for
Harmon Knitwear, 1973

Daywear

Left
Boldly patterned wool skirt
worn with a coordinated
striped sweater and matching
headscarf by Lanvin, 1973

Left
Printed cotton ensemble
comprising gathered
skirt, halter-neck blouse
with integrated tie waist,
a coordinated jacket and
matching cloche hat by
Lanvin, 1973

Daywear

Baby-blue mohair sleeveless cardigan
worn with a white silk blouse, wide-
legged blue linen trousers and pale
blue crocheted beret, 1972 – note the
"window wedgie" shoes by Shoe Biz

Opposite
Brown mohair quilted cardigan and
matching scarf-necked pullover worn
with wide-legged pants by Pertegaz of
Madrid, 1972

Right
Model wearing a purple pleated miniskirt,
a mustard-yellow jumper and patterned
silk neck scarf, 1970 – photographed by
Jamie Hodgson

Above
Patchwork patterned gipsy-style dress
worn with white lace-up boots, 1975

Above
Pink chiffon dress with embroidered and appliqué flowers worn with a
pink straw hat trimmed with silk flowers, pink tights and pink platform
clogs (left) and a red peasant-style dress with a floral printed bodice and
billowing sleeves worn with silver sandals, an artificial daisy choker and a
flower-trimmed straw hat, c.1975

Left
Model wearing flared jeans
with a cotton T-shirt, 1975

Opposite
Two models wearing flared
jeans by Wrangler, 1976

Daywear

Daywear

Above
The Parisian couturier André
Courrèges relaxing in his studio with
three models wearing clothing from
his 1971/1972 "Maille line" Winter
Collection, 1971

Jackets with short "teddy bear"
sleeves worn over knitted leotards and
accessorized with matching boots,
belt-bags, knitted gloves, caps and
large oversized sunglasses by André
Courrèges, 1972

Daywear

Opposite
White hooded "beach" cagoule with
drawstring waist and cuffs worn with
matching bikini and boots by André
Courrèges, 1972

Above
Two long-sleeved satin "Panta-
Riens" one-piece outfits worn
with "Toboggan" shoes by
Jacques Esterel, 1971

Above
"Rotten Row" all-in-one cotton playsuit with
drawstring waist worn with ankle socks and
wedged espadrilles by Mary Quant, 1975

Opposite
Natural beige Honan silk
pantsuit by Calvin Klein,
1973

Above
Green canvas trench coat worn with fedora (from
Joseph Magnin); navy-and-white vinyl jacket
worn with white turtleneck and white trousers
(from The Emporium); tan knit battle-jacket with
leather trim worn with plaid cotton trousers (from
Macy's), 1973

Opposite
Sarong-tied pants and matching
bandeau in plaid cotton with
reversible plaid/spotted jacket by
Anne Klein, 1973 – accessorized
with espadrilles and a wide-
brimmed straw hat

Opposite
Pinafore in striped ticking worn without
a shirt and accessorized with a wide-
brimmed straw hat by American fashion
designer Phyllis Sues – old-fashioned
uniforms worn by nannies inspired this
dress and its wide straps were designed
to be bra concealing

Above
Orange striped shorts and matching
jacket worn with an orange silk
blouse and accessorized with a
checked Arab-style headscarf and
brimmed hat by Wendy Dagworthy
and pleated silk satin embroidered
cotton halter-neck dress worn
with a wide metallic leather belt by
Marisa Martin, 1979

Right
Gipsy-style printed organza
"Rumba" dress with full sleeves
spilt from shoulder to wrist and
a gathered mid-length skirt
worn with Greek-style sandals
by Lanvin, 1970

Opposite
Red printed silk flannel smock
dress with oversized yoke by
Marimekko, 1972

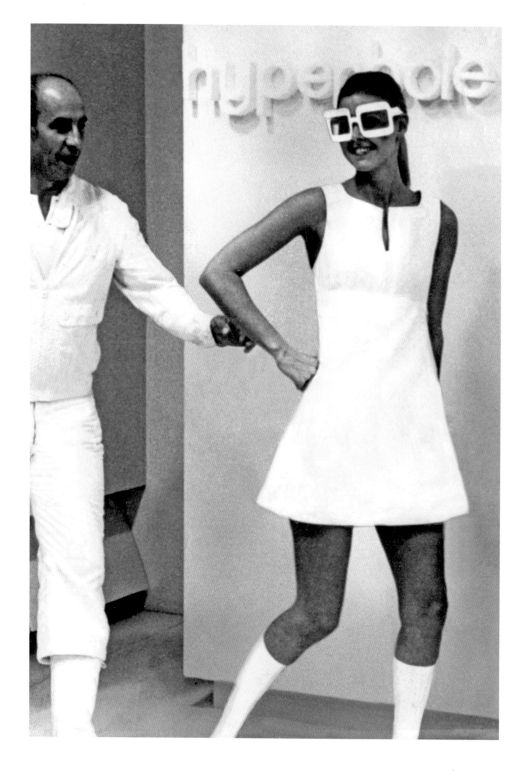

Above
White sleeveless cotton mini
dress with slit neckline worn with
oversized sunglasses by André
Courrèges for his Hyperbole label,
1973 – André Courrèges shown to
the left as one of his models takes
to the catwalk

Left
Red baseball jacket with cape
sleeves worn over a white shirt,
a black tank-top and pin-dot
flared trousers accessorized
with a matching spotted hat
and large oversized sunglasses
by André Courrèges, 1973 –
the jacket and tank-top bear
Courrèges's distinctive AC logo

Daywear

Above
Model wearing a cropped Hawaiian-style floral printed blouse with knitted cuffs and waistband, and jeans tied with a red scarf, 1973 – the Hawaiian theme is accentuated with the two large Hibiscus-style flowers worn in the hair

Opposite
Model wearing red hot pants, a white roll-neck jumper, a hip-hugging macramé-style belt and a crocheted cap, American, 1970 – photographed by H. Armstrong Roberts

Above
British model Twiggy sporting a
fashionable "page-boy" hairstyle
and wearing a cream buttoned shirt,
masculine-style cream flannel trousers,
a leather belt and men's spectator brown
and white leather shoes (especially
created for her by the legendary British
shoemaker George Cleverley), 1972

Opposite
British actress and model Joanna Lumley
posing in her role as "Purdey" in the adventure
TV series "The New Avengers" wearing maroon
banded cardigan, purple shirt and brown skirt
accessorized with a long pink-hued neck scarf
and tight-fitting boots, c.1976 – Lumley's "page-
boy" haircut was the height of fashion in the
early-to-mid-1970s

Right
Knitted dotted and striped
cashmere sweater worn with
silk shirt and black trousers by
Valentino, 1972

Opposite
Tight-fitting patterned woollen
sweater with matching knitted
cap paired with loose-fitting
camel trousers and camel coat
by Valentino, 1972

Honey-coloured beige cashmere
trousers with matching square-necked
camisole top and loose-fitting cocoon-
shaped jacket, 1972

Left
Tight-fitting woollen jersey
blouson with matching flared
trousers by Gideon Oberson,
1972

Left
Dot-patterned pleated top
with billowing rainbow-striped
sleeves worn over matching
loose-fitting pants by Issey
Miyake, 1972

Above left
Shiny black glazed cotton
tunic with lantern sleeves
worn over matching pants by
Issey Miyake, 1972 – note the
distinctly Oriental silhouette

Above right
Checked and striped pants
worn with matching blouse and
jacket and accessorized with
coordinated duffel bag and
shoes by Issey Miyake, 1972

Above
Beige silk linen suit worn with deep-collared blouse and matching hat by Oscar de la Renta, 1972 – note the monogrammed "R" belt buckle

Opposite
Shawl-collared brown Harris Tweed trouser-suit worn with patterned shirt by Ralph Lauren, 1972

Right
Norfolk-style pantsuit worn over a
turtleneck top and with a matching
brimmed hat by Ralph Lauren, 1972

Opposite
Blue velvet trouser suit worn with
satin blouse and grey flannel trouser
suit worn with a tricolour pullover and
brimmed hat by Jean Patou, 1972

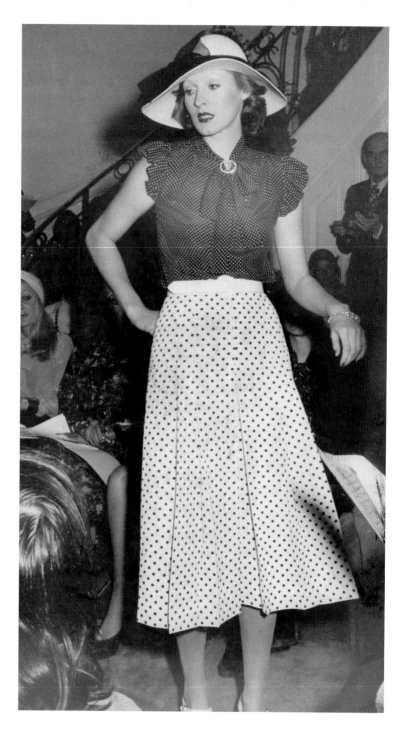

Above
Polka-dot patterned silk crepe skirt with ruffled
bow-necked blouse accessorized with a diamond
brooch, white leather belt and broad-brimmed
hat by Yves Saint Laurent, 1972 – inspired by the
glamorous look of Thirties fashion popularized by
Greta Garbo and other Hollywood starlets

Left
Cable-stitched string-knit twin-set worn with mid-calf-length bone-coloured jersey skirt and narrow waist-cinching belt by Oscar de la Renta, 1973

Opposite
Floral printed seersucker cotton two-piece outfit with smocked bodice and cuffs and two-piece gingham outfit with smocked shoulders, bodice and skirt waist by Adrienne Lemaux, 1972

Above
Orange dress with smocked midriff section worn with matching double-faced jacket by Philippe Venet, 1972

Left
Boldly striped tweed pants and jacket with pom-pom detailing worn with transparent silk blouse designed by Mitch Marsac as part of his "Franka Collection", 1972

Opposite
Pale green midriff-baring cropped sweater worn with poncho-style skirt and accessorized with a pale green suede turban and wedge sandals, 1972

Left
Halter-necked black silk crepe
cocktail dress slashed to the
waist and with high white
collar designed by Michel
Goma for Jean Patou, 1972
– accessorized with a triple
strand of random-sized pearls
and a wide-brimmed hat

Opposite
Ivory crepe shirtdress with
black banding and a pleated
skirt section by Caroline
Rohmer, 1972

Opposite
Pastel printed "shirtwaister"
dress in the sheerest wool
crepe with bow-tied neck and
matching wide-buckled belt by
Georges Reich, 1972

Above
Terylene polyester belted wrap
dress with a pattern of small
multi-hued blue squares set on
a white background by Michel
Pelta, 1973

Right
Dolman-sleeved white
cashmere sweater worn
with suede "umbrella" pants
and accessorized with a
matching cap and chunky
enameled necklace by
Pierre Cardin, 1972

Opposite
Grey suede flared trousers
by Anne Klein with an
angled hemline that is
longer at the back, 1972

Daywear

Left
Bottle-green suede dress with leg-o'mutton sleeves and taupe binding worn with matching stockings and high-heeled pumps by Jean Muir, 1972

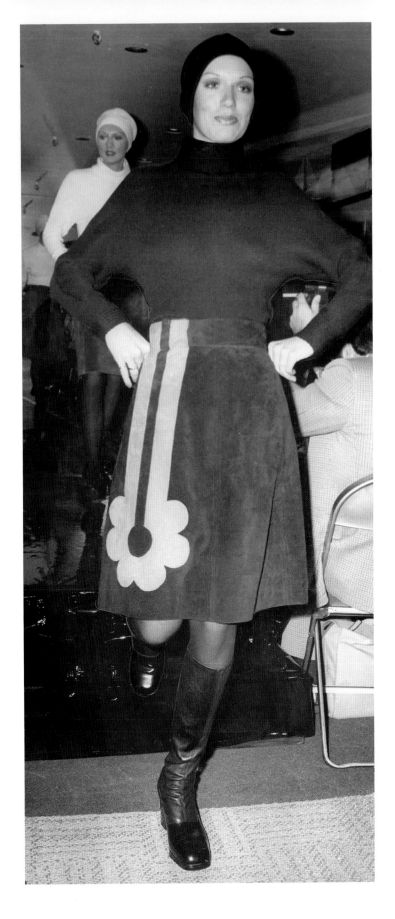

Right
Suede skirt with floral appliqué worn
with turtleneck seamed jumper,
matching cap and leather two-toned
boots by Pierre Cardin, 1972

Above
Sheer wool gabardine "Hydrangea"
print cape worn over matching silk
jersey dress in pink tones by Emilio
Pucci, 1972

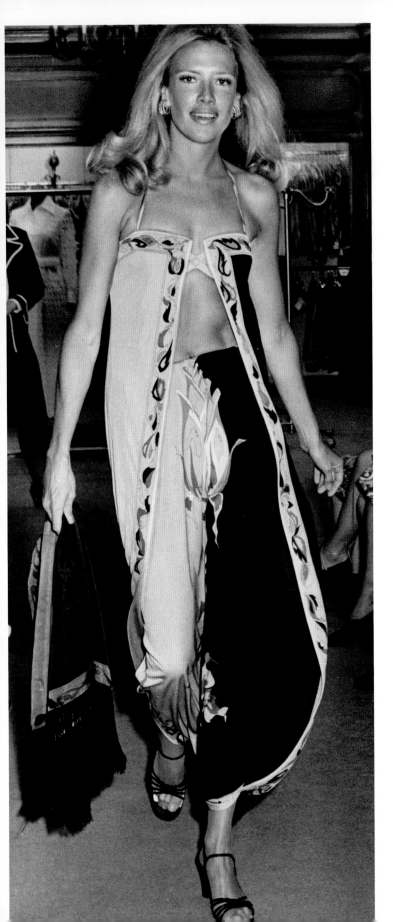

Left
"Rosebud" harem pants worn
with split-fronted evening top
in purple and turquoise and a
matching fringed silk stole by
Emilio Pucci, 1972

Daywear

Opposite
"Rosebud" harem pants in bittersweet orange and mocha brown with matching mandarin-necked long-sleeved top by Emilio Pucci, 1972

Below
Brown, beige and grey printed chiffon top with embroidered bands at the neck and waist worn with a matching long skirt slashed to the waist by Emilio Pucci, c.1970 – photographed by Franco Rubartelli

Left
High-waisted trousers worn with floral printed blouse, chequered knit cardigan with large buttons and a beret by Cacharel, 1972

Opposite
Floral printed wool crepe skirt worn with billowing sleeved blouse, tight-fitting waistcoat and close-fitted hat with large under-the-chin bow detail by Cacharel, 1974

Opposite
The Chambre Syndicale de la Couture
shows a dress and a trouser suit
ensemble as part of its presentation of
leading Paris couturiers' ready-to-wear
Spring/Summer 1974 collections held
at the George V hotel in Paris, 1973

Above
Red silk crepe shirt and wool skirt
worn with long knitted cardigan
by Vérique and a knitted zigzag-
patterned dress with bow-tied
neckline worn with a matching woollen
cardigan by Colette Jane, 1973

Daywear

Left
Daisy printed silk crepe dress with white sectioned collar worn with a hat adorned with artificial daisies by Yves Saint Laurent, 1974 – this design reflects the influence of 1930s tea dresses

Opposite
Daisy printed silk crepe dress with a swaying godet-panelled skirt worn with a horsehair hat by Yves Saint Laurent, 1973

Left
Brown-and-white checked silk-blend
shirt dress by Kasper, 1973 – inspired
by a dress produced by B.H. Wragge
from 1943

Opposite
Red, green and white striped halter
top and cardigan worn with white
sharkskin pleated skirt by Yves Saint
Laurent (left) and a V-necked cricket-
style jumper and white pleated skirt by
Ralph Lauren, 1973

Right
Bias-cut grey wool dress with
clingy bodice and full skirt by
Adèle Simpson, 1973

Opposite
Loosely fitted dress in navy
wool crepe by Fouks, 1974

Above
Navy-and-white herringbone tweed
suit with figure-hugging long jacket
and A-line knee-skimming skirt by
Adèle Simpson, 1972

Above
Collarless cotton foulard suit worn
with a bow-tied blouse, by Adèle
Simpson, 1972

Daywear

Left
Grey flannel jacket worn over
a grey-and-white tweed skirt
and a grey-and-white diagonal-
patterned crepe-de-chine blouse
by Christian Dior, 1974

Opposite
Forties-style three-piece suit
by Nina Ricci (left) and similarly
styled suit made using a Vogue
pattern from Dacron polyester and
Qiana nylon-silk (right), 1974

Opposite
Putty-coloured cotton
gabardine safari suit with
short-sleeved belted wrap
jacket and pleated knee-length
skirt by Victor Joris, 1973

Above
Safari suit with drawstring
gathered jacket and
knee-length skirt by Adèle
Simpson, 1972

Left
Black silk-knit halter-top worn with
long wrap skirt and matching scarf in
printed silk jersey and a large straw
hat by Adolfo, 1972

Opposite
Plaid jacket worn with duck-patterned
sweater, high-waisted navy slacks,
wide-brimmed straw hat and silk neck
scarf, American, 1972

Daywear

Above
An all-in-one ensemble in silk
and tulle with plunging back-
line by Hyacinthe Novak, 1972

Above
An après-ski ensemble in
green and gold lame worn with
a fox fur cape (left) and an all-
in-one pantsuit with plunging
back-line (right) – both by
Hyacinthe Novak, 1972

Above
Patterned polyester jersey tunic worn
over a turtleneck top and cinched with a
leather belt by Brettles, 1972

Opposite
Artificial "leather" mini skirts and
waistcoats worn with matching
blouses and hats (with same trimming)
and accessorized with tight-fittinng
leatherette boots by Marcelle, 1972

Daywear

Left
An example of British fashion
– all-in-one checked ensemble
with tie belt worn over a red
turtleneck top, 1972

Opposite
Knickerbockers worn with a
sleeveless pleated top and an
elasticized belt designed by the
London designer John Bates
(who designed under the *nom-de-plume* Jean Varon), 1973

Above
Autumn/Winter collection by
André Courrèges featuring
various jumper designs, 1972.

Opposite
Vinyl "battle" jacket
embellished with designer's
logo worn with a loosely
pleated skirt, patterned tights
and criss-cross tied sandals by
André Courrèges, 1972

Daywear

Left
Summer cotton tunic worn over matching trousers by Dorothy Perkins, 1974

Opposite
Tiered tent dress in terracotta-coloured crepe-de-chine adorned with a pastel floral pattern by Ossie Clark, 1972

Left
Wedding photograph of British football player Steven Cooper with his bride Pat, who wore a blue Lurex top, red knee-length jeans and black leather boots for her wedding at Brentwood Register Office in Essex, 1972

Opposite
Printed jacket with wide lapels worn over blouse and sweater and with hip-hugging flared trousers and cloglike platform shoes by Miguel Cruz, 1973

Left
Two trouser and blouse ensembles by Giorgio Armani shown at the Fiera Campionaria in Milan, 1979

Opposite
Brown glove-leather suit with wide elasticized waistband and worn with a matching brimmed cap and lace-up high-heeled shoes by Henry Lehr, 1973 – Henry Lehr had his own Soho boutique, which he moved from London to New York City in 1974

Right
American singer Madonna
modelling a long-sleeved
black top with a slashed
one-shoulder neckline,
tight-fitting jeans and high-
heeled boots, 1979

Opposite
American singer Debbie
Harry of the new-wave rock
band Blondie posing in a
"Patti Smith Group" T-shirt
and black thigh-length
leather boots, 1977 –
photographed by Duffy; the
moody insolence and overt
sexual suggestiveness of
the pose reflects the new
in-your-face ethos of punk

1970s Outerwear

Outerwear offered as much choice and variety as all other items in the fashionable Seventies wardrobe. Women could choose from a wide variety of styles, materials and lengths, either to match what was worn underneath or simply as a loud and proud statement of their individuality and identity.

While coats were favoured, because quite simply they are the most practical mode of outerwear, other items such as capes, capelets and fur stoles were equally fashionable. Coats, just like skirts, came in all lengths

Shorter jackets were mostly favoured for spring and autumn wear and came in a variety of styles, with both fitted and loose models being popular. References to earlier stylistic periods and designers were plentiful; late Forties and early Fifties jackets in the boxy style of Balenciaga were particularly popular for more formal occasions, while Thirties velvet capelets, originally designed as evening wear, were now popular for daywear. Short fitted denim jackets were perfect leisure outerwear and could be customized with patches and badges or more upmarket designer versions were available with a large appliqué designs on the back.

Short fur jackets, either real or faux, in Thirties style made a significant comeback too, although now often dyed in bright colours, a vogue for which had been initiated by Yves Saint Laurent at the start of the decade. Fur was also popular for longer styles, although its use was mostly limited to collar and cuff trims. Owing to its thick, rich pelt, fox was used liberally but cheaper pelts such as beaver, rabbit and squirrel were used as well, mostly on less costly items. It was also not unusual for cheap fur to be dyed to resemble more costly and/or more exotic pelts. While fur had always remained a staple of the elite's wardrobe, this association with an older conservative group meant that after the Second World War the young and hip did not particularly favour it, considering it to be a sign of elitism. In the Sixties, however, the popularity of second-hand shopping among young people had changed this attitude somewhat. Twenties and Thirties fur jackets now became playful dress-up items for those looking for an alternative to mainstream looks. Indeed, designer hippies marching down Kensington High Street in full-length fox fur coats topped with brightly coloured wide-brimmed hats became a common sight. By the 1970s, both the vogue for second-hand shopping and for historic referencing led to a more mainstream re-adoption of fur. However, unlike the conservative mink coats or tastefully ermine-trimmed jackets favoured by older ladies, the young went for big statement fur. Aside from (second-hand) fur jackets and coats with big fur collars, fur Cossack hats and big fur capes – often edged with fox or squirrel tails – were also popular. The styles of these coats varied greatly although whole fur coats often looked as if they had come straight out of a 1930s glamorous Hollywood starlet's wardrobe.

Fake fur was equally popular, especially in ready-to-wear fashions. Biba – and several other boutiques and labels that favoured the glamour styles of the Art Deco era – presented maxi coats of fake leopard and tiger print that matched the gauche dresses worn underneath. Biba also offered a range of capes in interesting colours and sizes. The cape, while not the most practical of items, became somewhat of a fashion hit owing to its dramatic quality during the Seventies. Both short and full-length versions were worn and were particularly suited to some of the more outrageous revivalist fashion styles that were popular throughout the decade; they were the perfect outerwear to finish off the peasant and the boho look on a colder day and also provided the perfect covering for a dramatic Thirties-style evening maxi dress.

Other styles of more dramatic outerwear featured Op Art designs of contrasting colour blocks and reflected the increasing merging between the art and the fashion worlds. For those who desired something less ostentatious, knitted coats were a stylish and comfortable alternative. Knitwear made a big comeback in the Seventies owing to a greater desire on women's part for unrestricted movement and thereby comfort. Knitted jackets came in a variety of lengths and styles, and were often created to match the knitted ensembles worn underneath them. The Italian knitwear label Missoni famously created some spectacularly multi-coloured knitted suit and jacket ensembles that perfectly combined the era's love of bright colours with elegance and sophistication. Textured knitwear was also used for jackets and long cardigans as it added the appearance of structure to an otherwise loose and relaxed garment. Knitted jackets tended to be belted, for the same reason.

In addition, more conservative tastes still were catered for by the wide variety of tweed and wool coats on the market. While the check was a rather traditional pattern, its application to contemporary modern styles updated its image and popularized it with the young and fashionable; checked flared trouser suits with matching belted jackets were for while pretty much *de rigueur*. Tweed also saw its image updated. Yves Saint Laurent's 1971 collection inspired by Forties fashions had re-popularized tweed with a younger audience. This traditional fabric was particularly favoured for more formal and work wear, and often coats were matched to suits. The shape of these jackets and coats tended to be borrowed from male tailoring, evidenced by the popularity for items such as the trench coat and the hacking jacket. This return to more traditional fabrics and an adoption of male tailoring for female work wear was typical of what would become known as the "Dress for Success" look. While in retrospect these fashions appear rather dull compared to some of the decade's wilder sartorial experiments, these suits and jackets were symbolic of the socio-political advances made by women throughout the decade and thus must be considered truly modern fashion items.

Left
Prince of Wales checked
coat worn over a tweed skirt
and roll-neck sweater and
accessorized with a grey felt
brimmed hat by Nina Ricci,
1972

Opposite
Plaid woollen coat with
sheepskin yoke worn with
tweed trousers and a matching
cap by Montreal-based fashion
designer Morty Garelick, 1972

Left
Pink wool three-quarter-
length coat worn over printed
shantung silk jacket-style
top and a pink shantung silk
pleated skirt by Emanuel
Ungaro, 1973

Right
Sporty evening ensemble
comprising tile-printed
silk skirt, drawstring-waist
sweater and a fur-collared
velvet jacket by Emanuel
Ungaro, 1973

Top left
Plaid trench coat worn over a moss-green and cream chevron knit two-piece outfit by Kasper, 1973 – in 1972, Kasper noted in the *Reading Eagle* newspaper: "Today's woman has moved away from freaky costume clothes and dramatic hemlines to classic sportswear. It's a mass reaction to the onslaught of 'nostalgic' clothes that the young find amusing and the mature consider old hat."

Top right
Raspberry-hued plaid skirt with side pleating worn with coordinated stripped jumper, cable-knit jacket, scarf and woollen hat by Missoni, 1973

Left
Knitted mini-cape (striped on the inside and plaid on the outside) worn over matching grey-and-black striped jumper and checked wool skirt by Missoni, 1973

Above left
British model Twiggy wearing a checked
Forties-style swagger coat with matching
trousers and accessorized with a felt hat
by Biba, 1973

Above right
British model Twiggy wearing a brown
chevron striped knitted coat with mouton
trim and accessorized with a tight-fitting
cloche-style hat by Biba, 1973

Left
White and brown wool coat
with large lapels worn with
a knitted brown bonnet
wrapped with an orange
silk demi-turban by Lanvin,
1972

Opposite
Trapeze-shaped cloak for
"young Soviet women",
French, 1973

Outerwear

Left
Black and white wavelike
patterned tweed coat with
a black fox collar by Hardy
Amies, 1972

Opposite
Soft lambskin coat with a
red fox collar and a leopard-
printed calf-leather coat
with a black fox collar by
Durer, 1972 – accessorized
with matching "reporter"
handbags and worn with
patent beige and black
platform boots and chunky
patent cinnamon and black
court shoes respectively

Outerwear

Above
Double-breasted black Saga mink
coat with brown leather lapels and
pockets worn with matching leather
cap and gloves by Frédéric Castet for
Christian Dior, 1972

Opposite
White astrakan "Swakara" coat with
horizontal banded inserts of white
mink by Jean-Paul Avizou for André
Sauzaie, 1972

Above
Parisian Street Style… Navy "Saint Laurent-style" jacket worn with jeans and a snap-brim khaki hat as seen on the streets of Saint-Germain-des-Prés, 1972

Opposite
Beige alpaca and wool blend tent coat worn over cream sweater and trousers by Donald Brooks, 1972 – shown with stylish Louis Vuitton luggage for the well-dressed traveller

Left
Long striped jacket worn
over striped top and pleated
skirt and in the background a
loose-fitting pea jacket with a
nautical "mail boat" patchwork
motif accessorized with red-
and-white striped tights by
Louis Féraud, 1972

Left
Long striped jacket worn over matching wide flared trousers and with a complementary striped shirt and scarf by Nina Ricci, 1973

Right
Two-piece trouser suit with
safari-style jacket from
Saks Fifth Avenue worn
under a double-breasted
herringbone wool coat from
Victor Magnin, 1972

Opposite
Checked tent-shaped
trench coat (reversible into
a poplin raincoat) worn over
a brown plaid two-piece
outfit by Chuck Howard,
1973 – Chuck Howard was
a pioneer of the "American
Look" in womenswear
during the 1960s and early
1970s

Opposite
Long white gabardine wool blouson
worn with matching trousers and
checked wool toile shirt by Armand
Fouks, 1974

Above left
Collared Tyrolean-style Loden cape worn
over green suede jacket, printed silk
blouse and tweed skirt and accessorized
with a heather-knit beanie hat by Yves
Saint Laurent, 1973

Above right
Embroidered jacket worn with
gathered woollen skirt, leather belt,
woollen scarf and chenille bonnet by
Yves Saint Laurent, 1974

Outerwear

Above
White double-faced short coat over green trouser
suit with double-breasted gathered-waist jacket by
Spanish fashion designer Pedro Rovira, 1972

Opposite
Reversible pink-and-white "windowpane" plaid coat
made of chinchilla cloth worn over matching trouser
suit by Spanish fashion designer Carmen Mir, 1972

Left
Maternity fashion: yellow
smock coat worn over
red trousers by Parisian
designer Dorothée Bis –
intended to hide the bump
of pregnancy

Opposite
Grey flannel trouser suit and
grey flannel belted capelet
coat by Givenchy, 1972

Above
Bold navy and white stretch
gabardine checkerboard jacket
with silk lining worn over navy
trousers by Givenchy, 1972

Opposite
White cashmere jacket based on the
theme of "Squaring the Circle" (using
two triangles and two rectangles)
worn over matching pants by Jacques
Esterel, 1972

Right
Drop-shoulder "topper" jacket worn over dungaree-style pant suit and roll-neck sweater by Geoffrey Beene, 1972 – accessorized with knitted "beanie" hat

Opposite
Hooded double-faced camelhair poncho with leather-buttoned side detail worn over green plaid printed suede trousers by Valentino, 1972

Opposite
Flaring waterproof cape-style
coat with godet panels worn
with a long woollen scarf and
brimmed hat by Jean Patou,
1974

Above
Reversible wool cape (with herringbone wool
cloth on one side and tweed on the other) worn
with matching tweed trousers and a smock-style
top in verdigris flannel by Philippe Venet for
Fouks, 1974

Outerwear

Above left
Fashion sketch of a grey jacket with stitched detailing worn over a white roll-neck sweater and white flared trousers by Mortone Vogue, 1970s

Above right
Fashion sketch of a faux leopard-skin driving coat with banded trim worn over a white roll-neck sweater and white flared trousers by Mortone Vogue, 1970s

MORTONE
VOGUE

68 Wells Street
London
W1P 3RB

MV 8119

Above
Fashion sketch of a green tailored three-quarter-length coat
worn over a purple roll-neck sweater and white flared trousers
by Mortone Vogue, 1970s

Outerwear

Above
Navy cashmere double-breasted coat worn
over cashmere pants and a high-collared
shirt and accessorized with a fringed scarf
and tight-fitting cap by Calvin Klein, 1973

Above
Rust fleece jacket with sewn-in handbag strap to prevent bag-snatching thieves by
Bonnie Cashin and sold through Saks Fifth Avenue, 1973

Left
Rust "space-dyed" knit cape with
red fox fur trim worn over a matching
two-piece suit by Adolfo, 1973 –
Cuban-born designer Adolfo Sardiña
established his own millinery salon
in New York in 1962 and then later
expanded into the design of women's-
wear collections, which were retailed
through Saks Fifth Avenue

Above
Forest-green mink short coat with a large collar worn over tweed
trousers and a roll-neck jumper by Daniel Hechter, 1973 –
opening his own boutique in 1962, the French designer Daniel
Hechter became well known internationally during the 1970s for
his creation of eminently wearable stylish yet sporty casual wear

Outerwear

246

Above
Hooded short-sleeved beaver jacket with
plaid pockets worn with satin trousers and
high-heeled leather boots and a fox poncho
worn with matching earmuffs, satin trousers
and high-heeled leather boots by Robert
Sack, 1976

Opposite
Australian actress and singer Olivia Newton-John
wearing a red fox jacket and matching hat along
with a pair of red trousers and black platform boots,
posing outside the Savoy Hotel in London, 1973

Outerwear

Opposite
Ivory wool ensemble comprising a
wrap coat with wide lapels, a four-
pocket quilted jacket with drawstring
waist and matching trousers worn
with checked silk scarf and turban, by
Emanuel Ungaro, 1972

Above
White dress made from
Dormeuil wool crepe gathered
at the waist with a belt and
worn under a bright yellow
alpaca wool double-faced coat
with "cape" sleeves by Guy
Laroche, 1973

Above
Four sports coats in bright orange, red
and yellow hues worn with matching
trousers or spats, and helmet-style
hats with goggle-like sunglasses by
Guy Laroche, 1971

Opposite
Short-sleeved tight-fitting black wool
coat worn with matching trousers,
white gloves, silk scarf and large
oversized sunglasses by André
Courrèges, 1973

Right
Woollen coat with brass toggles
worn over a roll-neck jumper and
plaid trousers by Kasper, 1972 – a
sophisticated reinterpretation of the
traditional duffel coat

Opposite
White double-breasted pea coat with
large sleeves gathered at the cuffs by
André Courrèges, 1974 – Courrèges's
highly tailored jackets, such as the one
shown here, became the blueprint for
numerous copies sold at every price
point

Left
Beige and white checked alpaca
wool and solid beige wool coat with
large wing collar by American fashion
designer Norman Norell, 1972

Opposite
Undyed griege wool knit coat with
raglan sleeves worn over almond-
green trousers and a striped V-neck
sweater and accessorized with a long
fringed knit scarf and matching pull-
on hat by Rodier, 1974

Above
British fashion designer Mary Quant (right) presenting
an ensemble from her "Northwest Passage" collection,
comprising a corduroy and mohair jacket, short cuffed
corduroy trousers, a printed wool shirt, a mohair shawl and
a "Mongolian" ear-flapped fur hat, 1975

Above
Three-quarter-length raincoat in light blue "Spinnaker" acrylic-coated polyester with a smock-gathered yoke worn over white turtleneck top and white flannel trousers and "Pivoine" (Peony) bomber jacket in black "Spinnaker" acrylic-coated polyester worn over a white turtleneck top and white flannel trousers by André Ledoux for his 1973 André Ledoux Sports collection, 1972

1970s Eveningwear

Eveningwear styles were arguably some of the most spectacular of the decade. In the first half of the decade, fantasy fashion ruled for both day- and eveningwear, but as the decade progressed more formal styles started to dominate daywear whereas eveningwear continued its flight of fancy. While mini and midi evening dresses were widely available, the decade's penchant for glamour firmly favoured maxi skirts and dresses above all other styles.

Evening dress was also the place where the historicist revival styles ruled. The most popular styles referenced the Thirties Hollywood glamour look of satin and silk bias-cut dresses. These historic styles were not mere copies of a bygone age; designers updated the look in a variety of ways. Many added in extra panels to create large butterfly capes and/or sleeves, while others deepened the décolletage to make them more racy and vampy. The main promoter of this Thirties style with a naughty twist was the London-based boutique Biba. Their fluid evening gowns often featured thigh-high splits and were often worn without a bra. These gowns retailed in all kinds of weird and wonderful colours and fabrics. Leopardskin was a particular favourite and was used liberally for evening coat-dresses. These Hollywood glamour-puss gowns were teamed with feather boas, velvet capelets and fur stoles.

Ostrich and marabou feathers, aside from their use in boas and stoles, were also often applied to evening dresses, again referencing costumes from Hollywood's golden age. The ostrich-trimmed dress worn by Ginger Rogers in *Top Hat* (1935) provided inspiration for many designers in the Seventies and various versions appeared on the catwalk. Thirties-inspired maxi dresses were equally available in bold modern prints in a wild range of colours. These dresses were a synthesis of Sixties' hippie styles and early-twentieth-century bohemian dress and were often referred to as "hippy chic". Zandra Rhodes and Ossie Clark were particularly known for their imaginative and original use of pattern and their dresses were the epitome of this polished hippy look.

Ethnic styles, so popular in daywear, also made an appearance in eveningwear, either through details such as embroidery and appliqué, or as actual garments. Kaftans, kimonos and djellabahs were made from diaphanous materials or given large side splits to Westernize them and, arguably, sexualize them. The peasant chic look was also translated into eveningwear through the use of belts and chokers with large artificial flowers and the addition of ruffles on dress skirts. While in daywear these skirts tended to be made of cheese cloth or cotton, peasant-style evening dresses favoured more conventionally luxurious materials such as satin,

or in the case of cheaper versions rayon. This romantic style also introduced a vogue for lace panelling, often on the dress bodice, but while in daywear the lace used in these prairie styles was white and oozed with innocence, the eveningwear counterpart tended to be black and consequently rather more risqué.

The growing popularity of disco music effected a diversification of eveningwear in the mid-Seventies as well, and introduced a less fussy and frivolous style that was still extravagant in cut but which lost the extensive detailing and the over-the-top prints. Fiorucci's skin-tight satin disco pants and brightly coloured catsuits are perfect examples of this new trend. American designer Halston was also at the forefront of this disco look, and his jersey and Ultrasuede creations were extensively worn by the glamorous set partying at the legendary Studio 54 nightclub in New York. The cut of his dresses was masterful and while appearing at times rather simple and unstructured, they were in fact carefully tailored to perfectly compliment the body in motion. His use of draping introduced a minor Grecian revival, especially within disco circles, which saw the popularization of long tubular-like gowns gathered at the shoulders and often slashed at the sides. Aside from his dresses, his jumpsuits and separates also became instant hits because they oozed glamour but were also really comfortable to wear.

Jumpsuits made of pliable and stretchy materials were popular eveningwear too. Daywear versions often featured long or capped sleeves, or were worn over blouses if they were halter-neck, but evening versions were much more revealing and favoured either spaghetti straps or halter-necks. Materials used for evening jumpsuits also tended to be more extravagant and glamorous. The late Seventies disco mania would see the body stocking or leotard, a more clingy and revealing version of the jumpsuit, become popular – especially among the young, who were more likely to have the body shape to stylishly pull them off. For those with a penchant for more conservative looks, knitted maxi dresses provided a viable alternative. Especially long-sleeved versions, which presented a fashionable yet more modest version of popular styles, while others could be teamed with matching cardigans that allowed the wearer the choice of whether to reveal or stay covered up. The clever use of capes attached to the backs of dresses had a similar effect and, furthermore, would flow and sway elegantly as the wearer danced. Elegance really is the keyword to sum up the majority of popular eveningwear styles that were introduced during the Seventies. For, however mad the print, the detailing or the accessories were, Seventies eveningwear ultimately presented more mature, polished and elegant versions of current daywear styles.

Right
British model Twiggy posing in an exotic
tent constructed in the photographer Justin
de Villeneuve's home in London, wearing a
heavily sequinned metallic gold dress with
matching turban and accessorized with gold
leather strappy shoes, 1972

Below
British model Twiggy wearing a faux-
leopard robe with matching hood
by Biba, 1971 — this photo shoot
by Justin de Villeneuve was taken
in Biba's extravagantly decorated
Kensington store

Below
British model Twiggy stretching out on
a leopard-skin bed in Biba's Kensington
store wearing a long pale gold satin
evening dress with matching long black-
banded jacket, 1971 – photographed by
Justin de Villeneuve

Right
Black wool and cotton dinner dress with billowing chiffon sleeves and a removable over-tunic by the Greek fashion designers Nikos and Taki, 1973 – the gold embroidery and chain-and-clip detailing reflected a fashionable Grecian influence

Opposite
Evening pantsuit by Yves Saint Laurent (left) shown with a similarly styled model made using a Vogue pattern and "Blue Ridge-Winkler" Qiana polyester fabric, 1974 – during the Seventies, home dress-making skills were still used by the vast majority of women to create affordable yet fashionable clothes for themselves and their families. For example the designer outfit here cost $2,068 to buy, whereas the pattern-made model cost only $37.23 to make

Eveningwear

Above
Tight-fitting camisole-top brown
evening dress worn under a floaty silk
chiffon poncho with a high-necked
green and beige frilled collar by
Valentino, 1977

Opposite
Knife-pleated gold chiffon Lurex evening gown with
an impressively full skirt by Donald Brooks, 1972 – the
American fashion designer Donald Brooks was cited by the
New York Times as being one of "the three B's of fashion"
alongside Bill Blass and Geoffrey Beene

Right
Purple and white print organza
evening gown with leg o' mutton
sleeves and worn with a matching
shawl by Lanvin, 1972

Opposite
Wine-coloured, hand-painted lace
evening dress with dolman sleeves by
Donald Brooks (left) and silk chiffon
caftan with a multicoloured floral print
set on a black background by Oscar
de la Renta (right), 1972

Opposite
Russet silk jersey wrap dress with padded
shoulders by Jean Muir, 1973 – worn with
a 1930s-style cloche hat adorned with a
large artificial silk flower

Above
Floaty silk smock-style top
worn over matching long skirt,
American, 1974 – accessorized
with high-heeled sandals

Opposite
Two "negligee-style" evening gowns with deeply plunging necklines by Jean Allen, 1974 – the one to the left is in black velvet and the one to the right is in satin; both incorporate lace detailing and have a large artificial silk rose worn at the waist

Below
Pleated chiffon two-piece evening ensemble with lace panel yoke and sleeves by Tiziani, 1974 – Texas-born couturier Evan "Buddy" Richards founded the Rome-based House of Tiziani in 1963

Right
Strappy tiered and pleated white crepe
evening dress by Donald Brooks, 1973

Opposite
Strappy black silk chiffon slip-dress
trimmed with marabou feathers by
Yves Saint Laurent, 1973

Above
Spotted evening dress with ruffle collar and cuffs,
photographed by Studio Press Holland, c.1974

Opposite
Crocheted long dress with matching shawl,
photographed by Studio Press Holland, c.1974

Eveningwear

Right
Coral silk poncho top with tasselled
fringing worn over white-tiered palazzo
pants and accessorized with matching
neck scarf, beaded belt and beaded
bracelet by Gucci, c.1970

Opposite
Cream silk blouse with pleated balloon
sleeves worn with embroidered
waistcoat, printed silk harem pants
and white patent shoes with gold
flowers by Valentino, c.1970

Eveningwear

Above
Café-au-lait silk halter-top worn over flaring trumpet-
style long silk skirt in three shades of blue retailed
by Joseph Magnin, 1973

Opposite
White fox-trimmed jacket worn over matching silk
crepe evening gown and jersey halter-neck evening
gown with a drawstring bodice and bias-cut skirt
accessorized with a white fox stole by Bill Blass for
his Resort and Spring Collection, 1973

Above
Peasant-style cornflower-blue taffeta midi
dress with deep tucked waistband tied
with a velvet ribbon and worn with laced
pumps by Givenchy, 1970

Above
Peasant-style geranium-red taffeta
evening dress with a patchwork-style
print worn with a long black velvet
chasuble-style sleeveless jacket tied
with black satin ribbons and laced
pumps by Givenchy, 1970

Eveningwear

Above
Spaghetti-strapped heavily beaded silver
evening top worn with a single strand of
gleaming pearls, a dark-coloured skirt, a suede
belt and a matching tight-fitting beaded cap by
Jules-François Crahay for Lanvin, 1972

Above
Pastel silk crepe evening dress with
plunging halter-neck worn with a fur
stole and an outsized pearl necklace
with a tear-drop pendant and matching
earrings by Marc Bohan for Dior, 1972

Eveningwear

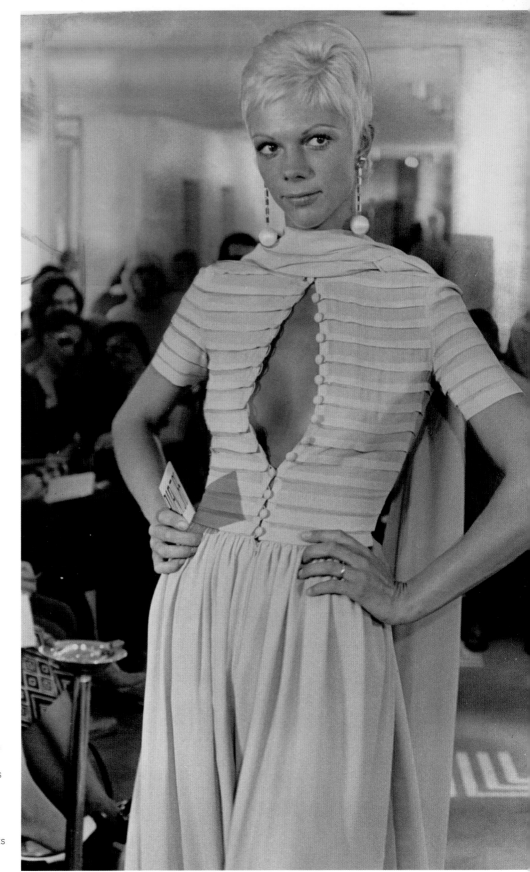

Left
Fluffy white angora "Panda"
kaftan with big red and black
dots and keyhole neckline, sold
through Saks Fifth Avenue,
1972

Opposite
Beige cashmere cardigan worn
over a brown satin evening
gown with bow-tied neckline
and diamanté-buckled belt by
Oscar de la Renta, 1972

Eveningwear

Right
Long evening dress with yellow
daffodil appliqués and two-tone
diamond-shaped belt intended
to created an optical vanishing
point to make the waistline
look smaller by Houston-based
designer Victor Costa for Suzy
Perette, 1972

Opposite
Russian-inspired hooded
evening dress by the Greek
fashion designer Yannis
Tseklenis 1972 – the initial "A"
in the print making reference to
Tsarina Alexandra

Above
Geometric-printed jersey evening
dress and culotte-dress by Jean Allen,
1972

Above
"Theine" yellow wool crepe "youthful sports" tunic dress worn over dark coloured shirt (left) and "Double Amour" pink and green silk crepe evening dress (right) – both by Michel Goma for Jean Patou, 1972

Left
Slinky brown jersey halter-
neck evening gown by
Oscar de la Renta, 1972

Opposite
Pale bone halter-neck evening
dress made of Qiana polyester
with a matching jacket by
Oscar de la Renta, 1972

Eveningwear

Below
Striped caramel silk and silver lame evening
trouser suit with the long "Maharaja-style" jacket
daringly fastened with a single button by Ted
Lapidus, 1977

Below
Pink chiffon and iridescent sequin
pantsuit with midriff-baring top and
matching jacket by Mollie Parnis
Boutique, 1974

Above
Black and white triangular-patterned
wool evening dress by Rudi Gernreich,
1972

Above
Slinky red synthetic silk evening dress
with lattice-patterned wool knit bodice by
Rudi Gernreich, 1972

Eveningwear

Above
Navy matte jersey evening dress worn under a long copper, red and navy sequined jacket by Mollie Parnis, 1973. Mollie Parnis was a doyenne of American fashion who, despite being born in the Lower East Side, went on to become a favourite designer of successive First Ladies and a regular attendee at the White House

Fashion sketch of a full-skirted evening gown with ruffled low-cut neckline by Oscar de la Renta, 1976 – accessorized with a large evening bag, chunky bracelets and large ring

Above
Two floral-printed cotton lozenge-formed "Jardin" evening dresses by Pierre Cardin, 1976

Opposite
Pale blue crepe evening wrap dress with puffy short sleeves and a ruffled neckline, American, 1972 – accessorized with bracelets made of pastel dice and a rhinestone hairclip

Above
Black crepe dress with lace sleeves, ruffled cuffs
and flowing skirt by Fabiani, 1973 – the Italian
designer Alberto Fabiani, who founded his own
couture house in Rome, was well known for his
skillful tailoring and trend innovations

Above
Blue and pink floral patterned
faille silk evening gown with
matching organza boa by
Givenchy, 1973

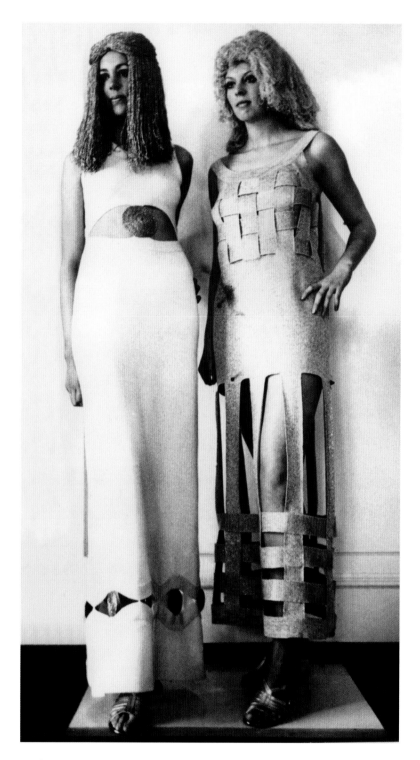

Above
White wool evening dress and yellow knit evening dress – both with body-revealing "windows" – designed by students from the Fashion School of the Hetzendorf Palace in Vienna, Austria, c.1973

Opposite
Fuchsia-pink chemise-style evening dress in sheer chiffon with applied circular motifs with metallic trim by André Courrèges, 1976

Above
Pink silk crepe V-necked blouse worn over a
navy pleated silk crepe long skirt and a navy silk
crepe halter-neck top with white banding worn
over a white silk crepe skirt – both by Yves Saint
Laurent, 1972

Opposite
Black crepe bandeau top worn with
draped long skirt and white crepe
jacket, 1972 – accessorized with a
black straw hat and strings of black
and white beads

Left
Azure blue silk top with
innovative padded "wing"
sleeves worn with matching
loose-fitting pants from the
"Il Futuro" collection by the
Milanese fashion house
Callaghan, 1978 – during
the late 1970s the young
Gianni Versace designed
for several Milan-based
fashion labels, including the
House of Callaghan

Opposite
Long yellow cashmere
sleeveless sweater dress
with matching sweater
tied around the waist by
Halston, 1972

Eveningwear

Above left
Two flowing long-sleeved diagonally striped evening dresses by the Milan-based fashion designer Biki, presented as part of her Autumn/Winter 1976 collection in Rome, 1976

Above right
Checked silk double-breasted evening jacket worn over long pleated skirt, Italian, c.1976

Above
Bustier and mid-calf-length skirt in delicate
Calais lace presented as part of the ready-to-
wear 1977 Summer Collections shown in Paris,
1976 – reflecting the influence of softer and
more feminine silhouettes during the late 1970s

Above right
Calais-lace bustier and mid-calf -ength skirt
presented as part of the ready-to-wear 1977
Summer Collections shown in Paris, 1976

"Document print" long dress by
the American fashion designer
Herbert Kasper, 1972 –
showing an Oriental influence
with its mandarin collar and
Chinese-style print

American actress and model
Candice Bergen wearing a red
cut-panne silk velvet kimono-
dress with Oriental-style
pattern by Bill Blass, 1970 –
photographed by Bert Stern

Left
Dolman-sleeved evening
chemise dress in cream wool
flannel belted with a chain of
golden balls and worn with a
matching necklace by Pierre
Cardin, 1972

Above left
Harlequin-print chiffon evening smock
worn over black velvet pants by Yves
Saint Laurent, 1972

Above right
Fashion sketch showing evening
ensemble comprising black silk blouson-
style top worn over matching pants with
banded rib-knit waist, cuffs and hem
sections by Pierre Cardin, 1973

Eveningwear

Eveningwear

Above
Long floral velour evening skirt with
black-and-white polka-dot georgette
blouse accessorized with a bow-style
belt adorned with a large artificial silk
rose by Hardy Amies, 1973

Above
Long floral-print skirt and
halter-neck top worn with
matching turban by Mary
Quant, 1973 – intended for the
beach and summer evenings

Above
Pink-and-grey checked long silk
taffeta dress worn under a blue velvet
and pink-trimmed waistcoat with frilled
collar by London fashion designer
Norman Hartnell, 1972

Above
Floral-printed pleated evening top-and-skirt
ensemble with asymmetrical one-shoulder
neckline and two-piece ensemble comprising a
boldly printed blouse and a godet panelled skirt
accessorized with a wide belt and matching beret
by John Bates (who designed under the *nom-de-
plume* Jean Varon), 1973

Eveningwear

Opposite
Long white evening dress with pleated
skirt and striped rib-knit navy and
white banding on the waist and cuffs,
and a long white cashmere dress and
sweater ensemble with maroon and
navy banding by Blassport (American
fashion designer Bill Blass's
sportswear line), 1973

Below
Two silk evening dresses with straight
skirts and kimono and mini-cape tops
in bold abstracted daisy prints by
Serge Lepage, 1975

Above
Floaty chiffon "Cascade"
evening gown with satin
bow-tied belt by Jean Varon
(the *nom-de-plume* of British
designer John Bates), 1973

Opposite
"The Painted Lady" evening kaftan by
Halston incorporating a batik-dyed textile
made by the South American artist Victor
Hugo, 1972 – Halston was instrumental
in making the kaftan fashionably chic
in the early 1970s

Above
Gauzy strapless evening dress
with a colourful rainbow-like
pattern by Pierre Cardin, 1979

Opposite
Salmon-pink chiffon evening gown with
a surplice neckline and marabou-feather
trimmed tiers by Valentino, 1974

Anti-static Ceylon jersey evening
dress with deep plunging V-neckline
by Kaiser, 1973 – model shown
barefoot in a London fountain,
reflecting a freer and more youthful
style of fashion photography

Opposite
Bright pink crepe sleeveless
evening dress with a pleated
tunic-style top falling from an
embroidered yoke by John
Bates, 1973

Left
Blue cotton print "Kabuki" evening
dress and another evening ensemble
with a shirt of the same material
twinned with a long blue skirt by Anne
Klein, 1974

Above
Luxurious Peasantry: peplum-
style red silk chiffon evening
dress with a gold floral bouquet
print by Yves Saint Laurent,
1973

Above
Wool and cotton evening tunic with
chiffon sleeves and gold embroidery
by Gump's of San Francisco, 1973 –
accessorized with jewellery by Achilles
and platform metallic-leather sandals

Above
Long dress with side slit in puckered cotton with
a multi-coloured print trim and a similar midi skirt
worn with matching top and scarf by the Greek
fashion designers Nikos and Taki, 1973 – both
ensembles were intended as "resort wear"

Eveningwear

Left
Heather-tweed wool cable-
knit evening skirt and top
ensemble by the American
fashion designer Hazel
Haire for Friedericks Sport,
1973

Right
Dark pink jacquard
geometric-patterned skirt
worn with high-collared
shirt and matching tight-
fitting woollen cardigan
by Givenchy, 1973 –
accessorized with chunky
Art Deco-style jewellery

1970s Accessories

The Seventies saw the adoption of accessories as diverse as its fashions for clothing. While certain wider trends such as the return of the hat or the platform shoe can be discerned, a woman's choice of accessories was as personal as the rest of her outfit, and thus handbags, shoes, glasses and jewellery came in a wide variety to accommodate all kinds of fashionable styles. While the decade is mostly remembered for its platform shoes, these were far from the only fashionable style available. Platforms seem to have grown out of the combination of late Sixties styles and a revival of Forties wedges. Available in a multitude of styles and colours, platforms could be found to match pretty much any outfit worn for any occasion. Perfectly in line with the fun fashions of the first half of the decade, they were however less compatible with the later and more conservative "Dress for Success" aesthetic. Working women, or those who merely adopted the look, preferred less clunky footwear, and opted for revivalist 1920s and '30s styles such as the "Mary Jane" or a simple court shoe.

Boots continued their late-Sixties popularity and were available in a host of materials, colours and styles. Classic leather boots with low heels complemented the Twenties-style skirt suits, while platform boots in bright or metallic leather worked well with hot pants, mini skirts or maxi dresses.

Platform boots may have been trendy, but unless a rather upmarket pair was purchased they could also be incredibly uncomfortable, hence a less extreme but equally funky boot with stacked heels was frequently favoured for daywear. These daywear styles were often made of suede or velvet and came in a wide variety of colours; Biba was known for its coveted plum- and leek-green-coloured styles.

Handbags could also be obtained in just about any style imaginable. Retro styles saw a host of historic bags return to the fashion stage: small Twenties compact cases, Thirties velvet pouches, more severe Forties square leather handbags and larger shoppers all complemented one look or another. Just as with shoes, there was a different type of bag to match every fashion look of the Seventies. While for evening wear smaller and more frivolous bags were favoured, daywear styles for working women tended to lean towards the more conservative: practical leather handbags that weren't too big to be imposing but weren't too small to be considered impractical either; the Success style wanted to convey an aura of respectability and seriousness and the bag was a major element of this. For leisure and everyday wear, straw shoppers and small leather bags with long straps were seen as convenient and stylish options.

During the Seventies, hats also made an unexpected return to mainstream fashion. Prior to the Second World War, the majority of women had worn hats to leave the house, but the war and changing societal conventions of propriety had put an end to this convention. During the post-war period, while some older women still retained the tradition, younger women had happily abandoned ornamental headgear. Sixties youth culture with its penchant for dressing-up had seen a renewed interest in millinery, in particular hats in historic styles, but it was only in the Seventies that hats – in all shapes and sizes – were wholeheartedly adopted again by the mainstream. Wide-brimmed felt and straw hats were particularly popular, especially after the release of the film of *The Great Gatsby*, which featured Mia Farrow as the beguiling Daisy Buchanan, dressed in a variety of romantic gauzy flower-trimmed models. Twenties-style cloche hats and berets were also popular and certainly a less ostentatious option.

In the latter part of the decade, the popularity of the less structured look meant that soft knitted hats, like knitted cardigans, wraps and jumpers, became increasingly fashionable. Fur hats, especially Russian styles, were also very much in vogue and added instant glamour to any outfit. When it was too warm for knitwear or fur, silk and rayon scarves were used to dress up an outfit, often wrapped around the head turban-style or draped around the neck 1920s flapper-style. Available in an infinite variety of styles, ranging from conservative abstract motifs and florals to brightly coloured bold psychedelic prints, there was literally a scarf for everyone. The "Dress for Success" fashion saw women use silk scarves as neckerchiefs in a bid to add severity and professionalism to their look by covering as much skin as possible.

Throughout the Seventies, glasses and sunglasses got bolder and bigger; large round frames were popular with, at the more conservative end of the spectrum, brown and beige frames being especially favoured. The young and funky in contrast adopted brightly coloured frames in a wide variety of prints inspired by Glam Rock acts, such as Elton John who famously accessorized his outrageous stage outfits with off-the-wall glasses. The fact that all different kinds of accessories were available in a plethora of styles directly mirrors the decade's wide and plentiful fashion landscape and shows just how individualized it had become.

Above
British model Patsy
Jones wearing pop
socks and platform
sandals, 1975

Opposite
Model wearing plaid tights by Amerex, red
wedge sandals by Capezio and a red mini
skirt by Getty Miller for Pranx, 1971 –
photographed by Rico Puhlmann

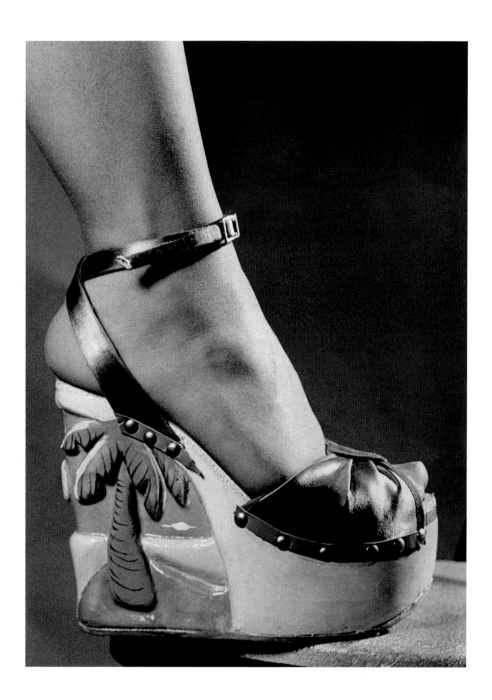

Above
Wedge platform sandal with high-relief palm-tree motif, 1975 – the early 1970s trend for "wedgies" was inspired by a growing nostalgia for 1940s and 1950s fashions

Opposite
Black leather platform sandal with winding leg strap and white leather platform sandal with daisy motifs by the Parisian shoe designer Roger Vivier, 1971

Opposite
Two pairs of sunglasses by
Jacques Esterel, 1973 – one with
a face-obscuring veil embellished
with small metallic pompoms and
the other with a crisscross of
threads over the lenses

Above
Sunglasses with hand-painted
zebra stripes by A. Maud, 1975

Accessories

Above
White fur Davy Crockett-style hat
by the London milliner Edward
Mann, 1975

Accessories

Cream sweater dress by Victor Costa
accessorized with a knitted cloche
adorned with metal clips, long cashmere
gloves, leather-covered bangles and three
strands of chunky beads, 1973

Accessories

Left
A cotton ensemble comprising
a striped and chequered
printed mini culotte skirt and
a waist-tied shirt with puff
sleeves embroidered with
flowers accessorized with a
matching "Peruvian" wide-
brimmed hat tied under the
chin by Louis Féraud, 1973

Opposite
Model wearing a white leather
"See-Through" hat with
flowered "goggles" by Jean
Barthet, 1971

Above
Printed ecru cotton shirt emblazoned with the "RBCC" logo worn with long navy and cream cardigan and cream trousers, and accessorized with a wide leather belt, alabaster beads, a chunky bracelet and a pith-helmet-style straw hat by Right Bank Clothing Company, 1973 – the Right Bank Clothing Company store was founded by Donald J. Pliner in 1971. Initially located on Campden Drive in Beverley Hills, it was one of the first American outlets for European designers such as Thierry Mugler, Castelbajac and Maud Frizon, and eventually went on to develop its own line of RBCC clothing

Above
Red V-neck sweater with navy stripes and trim and emblazoned with bold silver Lurex "RBCC" logo worn with a navy canvas hat by Right Bank Clothing Company, 1973

Opposite
A Stack of Hats – a variety of straw hats festooned with artificial flowers and embellished with ribbon bands presented by the Millinery Trade's Benevolent Association during Paris Fashion Week, 1973 – the year that Paris Fashion Week was officially launched

Right
White musketeer-style capeline hat
adorned with marabou feathers, a silk
rose and silk ribbon by the London
milliner, Edward Mann, 1972

Opposite
White leather pillbox hat adorned with
ostrich feathers and a leather rose by
the Parisian milliner Paulette, 1973

Below
"Britani" tri-coloured crocheted beret
embellished with a large ostrich
feather by the French milliner Jean-
Charles Brosseau, 1972

Opposite top
Daytime shoes and accessories, 1972 – rose-beige suede shoe with thick crepe sole, chunky ivory and gold necklace, yellow and white vinyl belt with eagle buckle and cream knitted gloves – all retailed by Joseph Magnin; bone-coloured suede clog, beige suede Mary Jane shoe, grey suede peep-toe pump, chunky gold and ivory necklace and a narrow vinyl belt – all retailed by Macy's

Opposite bottom
"Dressy Looks" for shoes and accessories, 1972 – pale grey and tortoiseshell clutch bag and rose-beige open-toed sling-back shoe – both retailed by Macy's; bone-coloured calf-leather handbag with green enamel clasp and beige silk evening shoulder bag – both by Gucci; pale grey strip sandal and pink, blue, grey and gold satin pump – both retailed by Joseph Magnin

Above
"Head to Toe" accessories, 1972 – yellow felt fedora hat, pale blue angora beret, ivory bangle – all retailed by Macy's; white mohair muffler scarf, chain necklace with perfume bottle pendant and a selection of pink and cream plastic bangles – all retailed by Joseph Magnin

Above
Pink and white straw hat (Macy's); washable yellow artificial
rose (I. Magnin); red and white spectator shoe (Saks); ebony
and silver bangle (I. Magnin); white and silver bangle and
pastel and pearl necklace (Saks), gold studded belt (I. Magnin),
multicoloured sandal, red and black pump and red and white
dotted scarf (Saks) – all from 1973

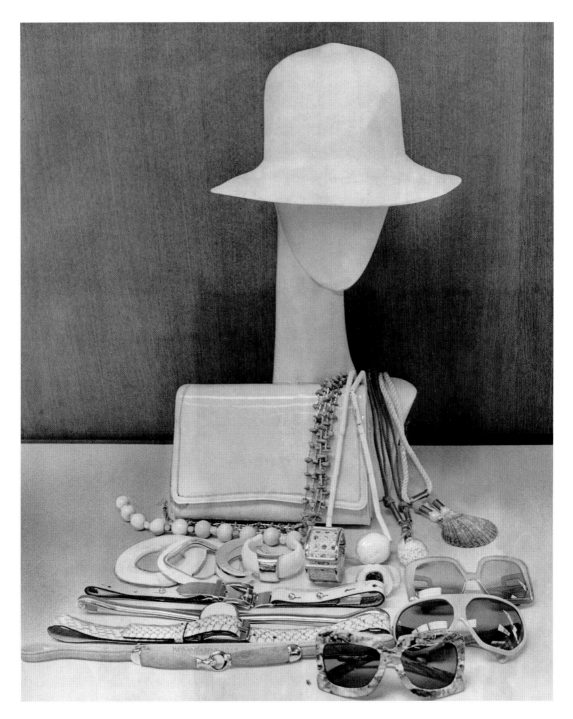

Above
Panama hat (Macy's); two shell and cord necklaces (Joseph Magnin);
ivory ball necklace (I. Magnin); turquoise and silver necklace by Zuni
(Saks); bone-coloured patent clutch handbag (Macy's); ivory slice
bangle by Halston (I. Magnin); ivory and gold bracelets, wicker bangle,
ivory and brown watch (Saks); ombre sunglasses by Dior (I. Magnin);
beige sunglasses by Yves Saint Laurent (Macy's); marled sunglasses
by Bernard Kayman (I. Magnin); bone-coloured patent belt with gold
buckle and ivory and gold snakeskin belt (Saks); snakeskin and suede
belt with gold buckle by Yves Saint Laurent (Macy's) – all from 1973

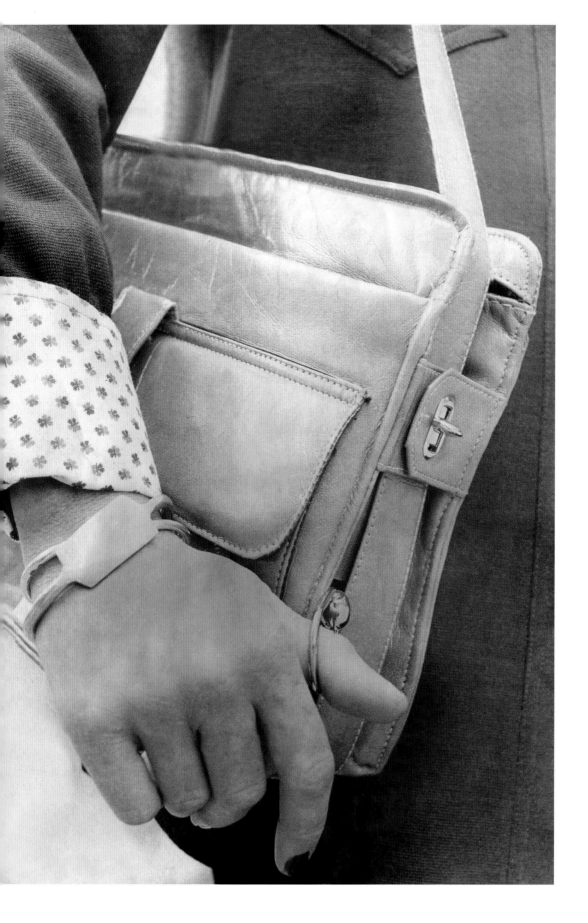

Left
Various leather handbags by
Pierre Cardin, 1972 – in red
and black, black and orange,
black and purple, yellow and
black, brown and green, and
black and blue

Opposite
Stop-Thief Fashion – leather
handbag with a gold ring
that when pulled sent out a
continuous alarm in order to foil
bag-snatchers, retailed by The
Emporium, 1973

Left
Beige brushed jersey dress
with coordinated jacquard
and knitted mesh jacket
accessorized with a double-
strand leather belt, a long
gold chain, a striped hat
and a long striped scarf by
Agnès B, 1978

Left
Simple tobacco-coloured
wool jersey dress with
peasant-style sleeves
accessorized with a silk
printed turban and chunky
bangles by Fouks, 1978

Left
"Halston in Acapulco"
– Black asymmetrical
swimsuit by Halston
accessorized with a
floppy black straw hat and
mirrored sunglasses, 1977

Opposite
American model Christie
Brinkley wearing a short-
sleeved checked shirt and
"Venetian-blind" sunglasses
by R&D Volpini, c.1973 –
Brinkley shot to worldwide
modelling fame during
the mid-to-late 1970s,
eventually becoming the
face of CoverGirl make-up
in 1976 (a position she
retained for 20 years) and
famously posing for the
cover of *Sports Illustrated*
in 1979

Right
Crystal earrings and ring by Dubaux worn with an evening dress by Calvin Klein, 1973

Opposite
American actress and model Anjelica Huston modelling chunky Aztec-style jewellery including rings, brooches, bangles and an oversized chain necklace by Schiavone, 1974

Above

A new masculine accessories fashion trend – outfit incorporating a men's-style checked shirt, a bow tie, braces and a waistcoat, Britain, 1977 – Graham Lack of the British Tie Manufacturers Association, commenting on the bow-tie trend seen increasingly in the collections of the Paris fashion houses as well as on the streets during the late 1970s, stated, "I wish women would leave this sacred emblem of malehood alone."

Opposite

The Shoulder Pad – striped silk jacket with tie belt worn with a close-fitting hat adorned with ostrich feathers shown at the Paris Fashion Show, 1978 – the outsized shoulder pads of this outfit reflected a move away from the free-flowing fashions of the early 1970s and towards the overtly masculine power-dressing look of the 1980s

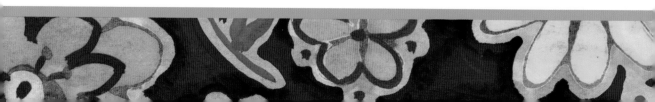

1970s Leisurewear & Other

Seventies fashion in general is characterized by increasing comfort. Not only through the adoption of easy loose-fitting dress styles, but also the use of more pliable and stretchy materials that allowed the body to move more freely than ever before. This was particularly noticeable in some of the most important leisurewear developments of the decade. Women's mass adoption of trousers came as a true liberation because it removed the need to constantly monitor one's body in order to make sure all was still elegant and in place. It also allowed easier engagement with leisure activities, such as cycling, as it removed the risk of accidently exposing too much flesh.

The popularization of jeans was possibly the biggest and most important fashion event of the decade. Denim jeans had originated in the nineteenth century as workwear for miners and cowboys owing to their rugged durability. After the Second World War, various subcultures such as bikers and later hippies appropriated jeans to signal defiance and a rejection of mainstream values. While these attitudes had already seen women adopting jeans, it was only in the Seventies that jeans shed their subcultural identity and became part of the mainstream male and female wardrobe. This truly unisex garment reflected a clear shift in gender relations and the breakdown of clearly drawn boundaries between the male and the female wardrobes.

Knitwear played a similarly central role within the design of leisurewear for similar reasons. Knitted fabrics such as jersey have a natural stretchiness to them, owing to their intrinsic structure, and thus follow the natural contours of the body rather than shaping them. This means that the body could move freely with the added bonus that, if made of wool or cotton, knitted fabrics are also breathable. Other less breathable but equally stretchy fabrics such as Lycra were likewise popular for similar reasons. It is this emphasis on the stretchy figure-hugging materials of the Seventies that often leads critics of the decade to condemn it as an age of overtly sexualized fashions, but what they often fail to consider is that aside from hugging the figure, these materials were extremely comfortable and were more likely adopted for this reason rather than to merely show off the body.

Showing off the body was nevertheless also part of Seventies culture because the time saw an increased involvement of both sexes in sport activities. Popular discourse on fitness and body image was increasing and, possibly in response to the popularity of these figure-hugging fashions, many women became aware of weight control. Fitness was now increasingly discussed in the female press and a growing number of women started attending work-out and aerobics classes in a bid to tone their bodies. These activities required specialized outfits and the colourful leotards, bodies and leggings worn for working-out soon crossed over into fashion and in particular leisurewear. Again their comfort cannot be ignored when assessing their popularity and adoption on a wider scale.

In line with this growing sports culture and body consciousness, beachwear became smaller, although not dramatically so compared to the previous decade. Both bikinis and swimsuits — often with cut-out sections — were popular holiday wear and came in a wide variety of colours and patterns, echoing the craze for both within daywear. Underwear also came in a plethora of styles to suit individual tastes. The bright and cute frilly girly modes of the Sixties remained popular, but were joined by more grown-up and luxurious styles in silk and satin that had a far more sexy demeanour. Likewise, pyjamas echoed the sensual boudoir wear of 1930s Hollywood as did silk kimonos, long flowing dressing gowns and full-length satin negligees.

Bridal fashions were very much in line with popular day- and evening-wear styles, but particularly favoured were the peasant and prairie looks, both of which had an inherent innocence of times gone by about them, making them ideal for a romantic wedding. As a bridal style, both featured lashings of lace, skirt ruffs and often high neck ruffs. Parisian designers tried to introduce a more sculpted and less fussy bridal look, one that was more closely aligned with 1930s decadence than the frontier spirit, but romanticism won — on a girl's special day, at least — and the peasant style remained resolutely popular for wedding dresses right up until the end of the decade and into the early years of 1980s, even though it had long disappeared from mainstream fashion.

Left
Cerise and white silk
crocheted jumper
and Bermuda shorts
by Serge Lapage,
1974

Right
Affordable fashions – red, white and blue star-print sweater worn with white denim tight-fitting shorts by WarmPants and retailed by Woolworths (left) and a "Kenzo-style" black and white epaulet sweater worn with violet knit trousers retailed by White Front (right) – these garments cost $3.99, $2.99, $7.97 and $9.67 respectively and reflected the increasing influence of high-end fashion trends on high-street fashion, 1972

Above
Two young Finnish models wearing sheer striped slip dresses stretch themselves in the summer sun, 1972 – Vuokko Eskolin-Nurmesniemi for Marimekko probably designed these youthful dresses

Opposite
White tatted linen ensemble comprising a camisole top, shorts and overshirt presented at Eden Roc in Cap d'Antibes by the Union des créateurs de la Mode Côte d'Azur as part of their 1974 Spring/Summer Collection show, 1973

Right
Model wearing a red and white patterned beach outfit comprising a halter-neck bikini and wrapover mini skirt, c.1975

Opposite
Model wearing a striped green and white crop top with matching hot pants and a Mexican-style belt, 1972 – photographed by Slim Aarons at the Las Brisas Hotel in Acapulco, Mexico

Leisurewear

Above
Orange plaid drawstring pants and
matching halter-neck top worn with
a duck-billed visor cap by Right Bank
Clothing Co., 1973

Above
White cotton Bermuda shorts worn with a
green and white striped shirt, heavy-knit
white cardigan and white knee socks (with
similar Bermuda shorts outfit shown to right)
by Valentino, 1973

Leisurewear

Opposite
Striped vest worn over Levi jeans with rolled-back cuffs and accessorized with a butcher's-boy cap, canvas tote and clogs, 1972 – according to the *San Francisco Examiner* this outfit reflected "Paris's roll-your-own fad"

Below
New Hiking Fashions – multi-coloured corduroy patch jacket worn over corduroy pants and accessorized with a canvas body pack by Abercrombie & Fitch, 1974. The man's outfit shown to the right is also by Abercrombie & Fitch

Opposite left
White cheesecloth pant
suit with multicoloured
smocking and buttons by
E.D. Jr, 1973

Opposite right
Bone-coloured chino pants
with integrated padded
seat outlined with double
stitching by Sonni, 1973 –
although intended to bring
a new level of comfort to
cyclists, this fashion idea
just didn't catch on

Left
Cyclist-print shirt worn over
bone-coloured chino pants
with snap fastenings on
ankles and a padded seat
for greater cycling safety
and comfort by Sonni
and pink halter-neck top
worn over pale blue pants
with a striped elasticized
waistband by Fritzi of
California, 1973

Left

Boho-Style Cruisewear: mint-and-white checked cotton tiered skirt worn with matching bikini by Canadian designer John Warden, 1973 – accessorized with wedge espadrilles and a large bead choker and matching earrings

Above
Three-piece ensemble comprising a
floral-sprig-printed cotton flounce-
hemmed wrap skirt, a halter-neck top
and a turban by Mary Quant for her 1974
Spring/Summer Collection, 1973

Above
Two "fishnet" tunics made from raw ecru cotton by Lazywear worn with metallic copper and silver leather ballet pumps by François Villon, 1978

Opposite
Slinky cotton jersey beach dress worn with a macramé-style belt by Leila for the "Sable et Soleil" (Sun and Sand) Collection, 1973

Right
Four customized entry
submissions to the Levi's
Denim Art Contest of
1974 – clockwise starting
from top left: denim shirt
and jeans embroidered
with elephant, fish and sun
motifs by Michael Young of
San Francisco; denim jacket
embellished with shells,
buttons and embroidered
chevrons by C. Kenneth
Havis of Denton, Texas;
denim jacket embroidered
with Native American eagle
motif and embellished with
flat metal studs by Beth
Pewther of San Francisco;
denim jacket embroidered
with an intricate seascape
and embellished with
shell discs by Constance
Comment of San Francisco

Opposite
Jungle scene embroidered
by Pamela Bernstein of
Eureka, California on to
the back of a denim jacket
and entered into the Levi's
Denim Art Contest of 1974

Above
Various bridal gowns modelled by
dancers from the Théâtre du Châtelet
in the gardens of the Sacré-Coeur in
Montmartre as part of the "Festival en
Blanc" held in Paris, 1974 – reflecting
the enduring popularity of floor-length
and very demure wedding gowns
during the 1970s, especially in France
and other Catholic countries

Opposite
Bridal gown in silk organdie with
delicate floral-sprig motif and large
circular cap sleeves worn with a
clustered rose headpiece and veil by
Serge Lapage, 1973

Above
Empire-line wedding dress in white organza
with a flocked apple-blossom print, ruffled
sleeves and ruffled collar by Emma Domb,
worn with a ruffled flower-trimmed organza
hat with integrated veil – both retailed by The
Emporium in San Francisco, 1974

Above
Empire-line wedding gown in guipure lace
with a flounced hemline and a large bertha
collar worn with a matching hat trimmed
with silk camellias and a cherry-red chiffon
bridesmaid dress with a ruffled capelet-style
bodice worn with a matching wide-brimmed
hat trimmed with a large silk rose – both by
Galina and retailed by I. Magnin, 1974

Left
Empire-line wedding dress
in white cotton voile with
capelet sleeves and a wide
lace-trimmed flounce worn
over a Breton lace hat with
long veil and a blue-and-
white checked daisy-
embroidered bridesmaid
dress with a removable
eyelet capelet worn with a
wide-brimmed lace hat – all
retailed by The Emporium in
San Francisco, 1974

N.163
Mod. LAUREEN

Sontuoso abito da sposa con originali maniche a campana e davantino a cappuccio. Guarnizioni di bellissimo ricamo.

Above
Illustration of "Laureen"
bridal gown with bell
sleeves and embroidered
detailing, worn with a veil by
Eva, Italy, c.1973

Left
"Monastic" bridal gown by
the Milan-based fashion
designer Biki, 1974

Opposite
Illustration of "Godula"
bridal gown with cape-like
train and worn with a pillbox
headdress with integrated
veil by Eva, Italy, c.1973

N. 253 Mod. Godula

Bellìssimo abito da sposa di linea severa, con ampio mantello sul dietro.

Left
High-necked bridal gown
with lace overlay on the
tiered skirt, bodice and
sleeves, and worn with
a matching headpiece
with integrated veil, *Ligne
Elegante*, Winter 1974/75

Opposite
Satin bridal gown with
stand-up collar, waistband
and hemline embroidered
with bands of pearls, worn
with a matching jacket and
a cascading veil, *Ligne
Elegante*, Winter 1971

Leisurewear

Left
Camellia-pink ruffled "Denise"
negligee with matching
nightgown by Brooks, 1973

Above
Pastel green "Discret" pyjama
set with wrap top in Dropnyl
jersey and trimmed with lace by
Lora, 1974

Left
American model Janice
Dickinson wearing an
oyster-coloured silk
dressing gown with a
knotted silk belt, 1978

Above
A lacy "baby doll" nightdress with
matching panties by Woolworths, 1974
– modelled by Beulah Hughes who was
Gossard's first Wonderbra girl at the age
of 18

Opposite
White silk and red lace push-up
bra with matching suspender
belt and panties, British, 1973

Leisurewear

Above
Model wearing a yellow
patterned Lycra cutout swimsuit
and another model wearing a
matching bikini, 1970 – shown in
sun-worshipping poses

Opposite
Model wearing a shiny brown bikini
lounges on an inflatable lilo, c.1970
– during the 1970s sun-worshipping
was a popular pursuit and resulting
dark tans were seen as highly
fashionable

Above
Maroon and white ski-racing
suit made from stretch nylon
and Lycra by Harris Meyer,
1972 – worn by the British
Olympic Alpine Ski Team at the
1972 Winter Olympic Games
held in Sapporo, Japan

Above
Waterproof nylon ski jacket with Belle
Époque poster print and acrylic fur
collar worn over matching stretch
nylon ski pants and with a knitted ski
hat, France, 1974 – the male model
also wears a waterproof ski jacket in
three hues of blue

Above
Beige waterproof poplin sports parka with red fox-trimmed hood worn over flannel trousers by Yves Saint Laurent, 1973

Left
Glossy black vinyl zippered ski jacket worn over stretch ski pants and with matching hat and boots by Givenchy, 1972

Leisurewear

Above
Red, green and blue ski jacket
worn with red ski pants by
Bogner, c.1972 – accessorized
with a blue knit hat by Glentex
and an "Olympic Timer"
watch by Lafayette Watch
– photographed by Mike
Reinhardt

Opposite
Red ski jacket (shaped like a
bush jacket) worn over blue
ski overalls by Globe of New
Hampshire and accessorized
with a wide red headband and
metal-framed sunglasses,
c.1972 – photographed by
Mike Reinhardt

BIOGRAPHIES

Adolfo
American Fashion House (1962–93)
Born in Cuba, Adolfo F. Sardiña emigrated to New York in 1948 and the same year became a millinery designer for Bergdorf Goodman. Between 1950 and 1952 he was apprenticed as a milliner at the salon of Cristobal Balenciaga in Paris, and between 1951 and 1958 also designed hats under the name "Adolfo of Emmé" for Bergdorf Goodman. In 1958 he became an American citizen and four years later founded his own millinery salon in New York, which later expanded to include womenswear. From 1978 he also produced the "Adolfo Menswear" range and the "Adolfo Scarves" line, and launched his own "Adolfo" perfume. In 1993 his fashion workroom was closed in order to concentrate on licensing deals.

Jean Barthet
French milliner (1930–2000)
Born in the French Pyrénées, Jean Barthet moved to Paris in 1947 and two years later launched his first millinery collection. His reputation grew over the following years and by the 1960s he was one of the leading Parisian milliners, his clientele including numerous film stars. As a member of the Chambre Syndicale de la Couture Parisienne, he also worked with numerous fashion designers, including Sonia Rykiel, Emanuel Ungaro, Claude Montana and Karl Lagerfeld, providing stylishly innovative hats for their collections.

Biba
British fashion label (founded 1963)
Biba was set up by the designer Barbara Hulanicki with her husband Stephen Fitz-Simon as a mail order company in 1963 to retail her Art Nouveau-inspired clothes. The following year, Biba's pink gingham dress with a matching headscarf was featured in *The Daily Mirror*, which led to an astonishing 17,000 sales. Also in 1964, the first Biba boutique was opened in Abingdon Road, Kensington, which then moved to Kensington Church Street in 1966. Described by *Time* magazine that year as "the most 'in' shop" for girls, Biba's dramatic rise led to a further expansion in 1969, with the boutique taking over a department store premises in Kensington High Street. This emporium became a "destination" for the fashionably informed and in 1970 the hugely popular Biba cosmetics line was launched. The financial downturn of the mid-1970s forced the store's closure in 1975. Two years later the Biba name was sold, but in 2006 the label was successfully re-launched by Michael Pearce and is now exclusively retailed through House of Fraser.

Bill Blass
American Fashion Designer (1922–2002)
Bill Blass began his design career making Hollywood-inspired gowns at the age of 15, which he then sold to a New York manufacturer for $25 each. The proceeds enabled him to study fashion design at Parson's School of Design in 1939. He subsequently worked as a sketch artist for David Crystal Sportswear in New York and in 1945 he became a designer for Anna Miller and Company in New York. He later joined Maurice Rentner Ltd in 1959, first as a designer and then two years later became its vice-president. In 1970 he purchased the venture and renamed it Bill Blass Ltd, introducing the popular Blassport sportswear line in 1972. In 1978 he launched his own signature perfume and during the coming years began successfully to license his designs for womenswear and menswear as well as for furs, shoes, swimwear, bed linens, jeans and luggage. After suffering a mild stroke in 1998, he sold his company the following year and in 2000 created his last collection.

Marc Bohan
French fashion designer (1926–)
Marc Bohan was encouraged to become a fashion designer by his mother, who was herself a milliner. After leaving school, he worked for the Parisian fashion designer Roger Piguet for four years before becoming an assistant to Edward Molyneux in 1949. He later worked as a designer for Madeleine de Rauch in 1952 and in 1953 opened his own short-lived Paris salon, which produced just one collection. In 1954, Bohan moved to Jean Patou, where he was responsible for designing the fashion house's Haute Couture collection. In 1958, he left Jean Patou in order to become a designer for Christian Dior. Two years later, Bohan replaced Yves Saint Laurent as Christian Dior's creative director, a position he retained until 1989. During this tenure Bohan created numerous collections that elegantly channelled contemporary influences into a definable Dior look. In 1990, Bohan was persuaded to join the floundering London-based fashion house of Norman Hartnell, where he remained until 1992 when the firm closed. After this, Bohan designed under his own name.

Donald Brooks
American fashion designer (1928–2005)
Donald Brooks (born Donald Marc Blumberg) studied fine art before deciding to become a costume and fashion designer. To this end, he studied at the Fashion Institute of Technology and later at Parson's School of Design. Brooks's first entrée into the fashion world was as a window designer for Lord & Taylor – his work caught the attention of the department store's president, who subsequently hired him as a fashion designer. In 1958 Brooks began designing sportswear for Townley Frocks and with the backing of the manufacturer Ben Shaw launched the first collection designed under his own name in 1965. Around this time, he opened his own store and his reputation grew to such an extent that he was described by *The New York Times* as one of "the three Bs of fashion" alongside Geoffrey Beene and Bill Blass. Apart from his elegant fashion collections, Brooks also designed costumes for more than twenty Broadway shows.

Cacharel
French fashion house (founded 1964)
The fashion designer Jean Bousquet launched the Cacharel brand in 1962, and two years later established a company of the same name. During the 1960s and 1970s, Cacharel's collections were notable for their youthful, airy femininity – as they are still today. In 1978, the house launched in collaboration with L'Oréal its hugely popular Anaïs Anaïs perfume.

Pierre Cardin
Italian-born French fashion designer (1922–)
Pierre Cardin began his fashion career working as a clothier's apprentice at the tender age of 14 and then later worked for a tailor. After the Second World War, he moved to Paris and worked at the Paquin fashion house and also with Elsa Schiaparelli. In 1947, he became head of Christian Dior's tailoring studio and then three years later established his own fashion house, which was launched with a masquerade ball in Venice. During the 1960s he became famous for his avant-garde Space Age creations and in 1971 he opened the Espace Cardin, a cultural centre that he also used as a venue to show his collections. Cardin was one of the first designers to extensively license his name, and in 1968 extended this activity to also cover a wide range of consumer goods including homewares and luggage. He was also one of the first designers to hold fashion shows in Asia and opened stores not only there but across the world – thereby helping to promote the globalization of fashion and ultimately luxury brands.

Ossie Clark
British fashion designer (1942–96)
Raymond "Ossie" Clark was a hugely influential British fashion designer during the 1960s and 1970s. While studying at the Royal College of Art, he lived with the textile designer Celia Birtwell, and after he graduated in 1965 the duo collaborated on their first collection for their Quorum boutique in London, which was shown the following year. The pair are credited with inventing the modern catwalk show by not only introducing music to such events but also inviting London's glitterati to attend them. Clark's skilful cutting of flamboyant garments which were influenced by both Hollywood glamour and Pop Art, combined with Birtwell's understand of pattern and texture, ensured the creation of designs that were not only highly innovative but also eminently wearable. Despite this, their Quorum fashion label floundered financially and was eventually taken over in 1967 by Radley, which expanded its retail operations and introduced various diffusion lines, including "Ossie Clark for Radley".

André Courrèges
French fashion designer (1923–)
André Courrèges studied engineering prior to training as a fashion and textile designer. He later worked for Balenciaga, where he learnt how to skilfully cut garments.

In 1961 he opened his own fashion house, where he pioneered a youthful and futuristic "Space Age" look that had a distinctive astronaut quality about it, and he often accessorized his angular silver and white outfits with flat boots, goggles and helmets. Often credited alongside Mary Quant as the inventor of the mini skirt, he was also instrumental in the increasing acceptance of trousers worn as daywear. He was noted for his signature tennis dresses and sailor dresses. During the 1970s he designed a number of more accessible diffusion lines. Today, the Courrèges fashion house still creates clothes with a youthful Sixties sensibility, while having, like so many other fashion houses, also diversified into the creation of accessories, luggage and perfume.

Oscar de la Renta
Dominican-born American fashion designer (1932–)
Born in the Dominican Republic, Oscar de la Renta studied painting in Madrid and then later apprenticed with Cristóbal Balenciaga, whom he considered his mentor. He subsequently worked for Lanvin in Paris, and later for Elizabeth Arden on the advice of *Vogue* editor-in-chief Diana Vreeland. In 1965, he launched his own label, which became renowned for its elegant Couture-style ready-to-wear collections. Between 1993 and 2003, he also designed the Haute Couture collections for the French fashion house Balmain, and in 2006 his own label successfully diversified into bridal wear.

Jacques Esterel
French fashion designer (1917–74)
Born Charles Martin, Jacques Esterel was not only a fashion designer but also a singer and composer. In 1953 he founded his own eponymous fashion house and six years later designed the pink gingham "Vicky" gown worn by Brigitte Bardot for her marriage to Jacques Charrier. During the 1960s and 1970s he referenced emerging street styles in his collections and also launched a "unisex" line in 1970 that comprised matching his and her outfits.

Louis Féraud
French fashion designer (1921–99)
Louis Féraud opened his first couture boutique in Cannes in 1950 and then five years later founded his own fashion house in Paris, which produced ready-to-wear collections. In 1958, he introduced his first Haute Couture collection and later in 1970 began designing popular ready-to-wear collections for the German-based fashion house Fink. He diversified into menswear and sportswear in 1975 and 1989 respectively. During the 1980s he became celebrated for designing the glamorous power-dressing gowns worn by actresses in the popular television series *Dynasty* and *Dallas*. His house continued to operate after his death in 1999, and since 2006 Jean Pierre Marty has been its creative director.

Rudi Gernreich

Austrian-born American fashion designer (1922–85)
Rudi Gernreich invented the topless monokini that was
famously modelled by Peggy Moffitt in 1964 and also the
same year created the first transparent "no bra" bra. Having
previously worked as a swimwear and shoe designer, he
had founded his own Los Angeles-based company, GR
Designs, in 1960, which was renamed Rudi Gernreich Inc.
in 1964. Two years later, his clothes were featured in what
is generally believed to be the first fashion video, *Basic
Black*, which was directed by his long-time collaborator
William Claxton. During the 1970s Gernreich continued
to create highly avant-garde clothes that often referenced
contemporary Op Art trends and also produced matching
his and her "unisex" ranges as well as creating Oriental-
inspired collections for Harmon Knitwear.

Bill Gibb

British fashion designer (1944–88)
Bill Gibb trained at Saint Martin's School of Art before
winning a scholarship to the Royal College of Art. However,
he left before the completion of studies to launch his own
company in 1972. Three years later he opened his first
shop in Bond Street and in 1970 the "Bill Gibb Room"
was opened in Harrods department store. His historically
inspired clothes epitomized the emerging romantic
eclecticism of the 1970s and often were co-designed with
the textile designer Kaffe Fasset. Despite critical acclaim,
his business floundered during the late 1970s and during
the 1980s he created only small capsule collections and
designs for a select private clientele, while licensing his
name to other manufacturers.

Michel Goma

French fashion designer (active 1960s & 1970s)
After studying dressmaking, Michel Goma moved to
Paris and worked for the house of Jeanne Lafaurie. He
acquired the business in 1958 and subsequently renamed
it Michel Goma. He closed this venture in 1963 and the
same year became a designer for Jean Patou. In 1975, he
re-established his own label and later worked as a designer
for the Japanese department store Isetan.

Halston (Roy Halston Frowick)

American fashion designer (1932–90)
Although born Roy Halston Frowick, the Iowa-born fashion
designer was simply known as "Halston". He initially studied
fashion illustration at The Art Institute of Chicago, before
commencing his career as a hat designer for the legendary
milliner Lilly Daché. He later left Daché to become head
milliner for the Bergdorf Goodman department store.
One of his most notable hat designs was the large cream
pillbox hat worn by Jacqueline Kennedy for her husband's
inauguration in 1961. Five years later he created his first
womenswear collection for Bergdorf Goodman, and this
was followed in 1968 by the launch of his first "Halston"
collection. He soon became famous for his easy-to-wear

yet elegant garments, which often utilized in their design
Ultrasuede and fine jersey knits, with *Newsweek* describing
him as "the premier fashion designer of all America". He
also successfully launched his own eponymous perfume,
the teardrop-shaped bottle of which was designed by Elsa
Peretti. In 1983, he signed a partnership with J.C. Penney,
which many felt led to the debasement of the label. Since
his death in 1990, there have been several attempts to
revive his fashion label – which during the 1970s had been
synonymous with glamorous fashionability.

Daniel Hechter

French fashion designer (1938–)
Daniel Hecher could be said to have been born into fashion
for his family owned a ready-to-wear firm and thus he was
brought up in the midst of the fashion industry. He began
designing his own fashions during the late 1950s, which
were sold by both Louis Férard and Jacques Esterel. In
1962, he founded his own eponymous label and the same
year opened his first boutique, which became known for its
wearable yet stylish sportswear. In 1971, he became one of
the first designers to create skiing and tennis ranges and in
1989 he launched his first perfume. During the 1970s and
1980s, his company expanded rapidly into an international
recognized *prêt-a-porter* label and continues to this day
producing sporty yet stylish clothes.

Betsey Johnson

American fashion designer (1942–)
The American fashion designer Betsey Johnson studied
at the Pratt Institute and then interned at *Mademoiselle*
magazine. She subsequently worked as a designer for
the Manhattan boutique Paraphernalia and around the
same time became associated with the scene surrounding
Andy Warhol's Factory as well as the "youthquake" fashion
movement. In 1969, she opened her own boutique, Betsey
Bunky Nini, in New York, with the actress Edie Sedgwick
becoming her house model. During the 1970s she started
her own fashion label, which became famous for its
whimsical over-the-top designs that were inspired by her
love of costume and also channelled the new and emerging
punk zeitgeist. Since then her company has expanded to
comprise 45 boutiques in America, Canada and Britain.

Anne Klein

American fashion designer (1921–74)
Anne Klein was born in Brooklyn in 1921 and changed
her name from Hannah Golofski while still a teenager.
She attended the Traphagen School of Fashion and at the
age of 15 began working as a fashion sketcher. In 1939,
she became a junior designer for Vardin Petites and in
1948 established her own company, Junior Sophisticates.
Together with her second husband, she founded the
popular Anne Klein label in 1968. Renowned for her easy-
to-wear, mix-and-match separates, Klein also designed a
girdle specifically to wear under mini skirts. She was twice
the recipient of the Neiman Marcus Award for fashion

leadership, and both Donna Karan and Louis Dell'Olio designed for her label and later took over its creative direction following her death.

Calvin Klein
American fashion designer (1942–)
Calvin Klein studied at New York's Fashion Institute of Technology and later established his own company in 1968. Klein subsequently created a range of coats and suits that caught the eye of the buyer at Bonwit Teller, which in turn led to support from the store's then-president. The fashion publicist Eleanor Lambert, who helped to shape his early career, also helped him establish a strong position within the fashion industry. Pioneering a distinctive "American Look", Klein incorporated elements found in active sports clothing into his casual yet elegant sportswear garments. Extremely business-savvy, Klein was the first designer to introduce jeans onto the catwalk. He also understood the power of advertising and memorably ran the ad campaign for his skin-tight jeans featuring the young Brooke Shields asking, "Want to know what comes between me and my Calvins? Nothing." During the 1980s Klein launched his commercially successful underwear lines for both men and women and also introduced the first of his many perfumes, "Obsession", in 1985. Today, Klein's impressive fashion empire also includes various non-fashion product ranges and is marketed through a plethora of licensees.

Ted Lapidus
French fashion designer (1929–2008)
The son of a Russian-Jewish émigré tailor, Edmond "Ted" Lapidus studied fashion design before working for the House of Dior, from 1949 to 1951. In 1951 he launched his own label and six years later opened his own Haute Couture salon. He launched his first collection in 1963 and the same year signed an agreement to provide affordable ready-to-wear garments to La Belle Jardinière, a chain of low-priced fashion stores. During the 1970s he branched out into the design of accessories and in 1974 opened a boutique in New York. Credited with making high fashion looks accessible to the average woman and man on the street, Lapidus was also an influential pioneer of the unisex look and was instrumental in popularizing the safari suit in the 1970s.

Ralph Lauren
American fashion designer (1939–)
The Bronx-born son of Ashkenazi Jewish immigrants, Ralph Rueben Lifshitz embraced the American dream and as *Vogue* put it "made it look even better". Having studied business and served in the military, Lauren opened his first tie shop in 1967. He then began designing stylish preppy menswear and in 1971 introduced his own women's label. In 1974, he was asked to design suave men's costumes for the film *The Great Gatsby*, which cemented his own distinct fashion look and helped build his reputation considerably. In 1978, the launch of his influential Westernwear collections

for both men and women, which drew inspiration from American heritage, kicked off a new Western style trend. Over the years, he went on to expand his design remit to include sportswear, casual wear and homewares. Importantly he was one of the first designers to understand the concept of lifestyle branding, once stating, "We don't only sell clothes, we are selling a dream and a vision." Today his company is one of the leading global fashion brands, which sells not only an astounding number of products but also alluring lifestyle associations.

Levi Strauss & Co.
American clothing brand (founded 1853)
Established in the mid-nineteenth century, Levi Strauss & Co. is one of the world's most recognized jeans brands. The company experienced significant growth during the 1960s, when jeans made from the transition from workwear and biker gear to a must-have clothing item for the counter-culture youth generation. The 1970s "blue jeans craze" saw Levi's introduce various new models of jeans and other garments and undergo further rapid expansion, with its manufacturing capacity expanding from 16 to 63 plants in the USA and a further 23 overseas opening between 1964 and 1974. During the early 1970s, the company ran a popular ad campaign with the memorable byline "Have you ever had a bad time in Levi's?".

Missoni
Italian fashion house (founded 1953)
Ottavio and Rosita Missoni founded the Italian fashion house Missoni in Varese in 1953. Initially they concentrated on the production of knitted ready-to-wear clothing and during the early years collaborated with the Biki boutique in Milan, working with its manager on collections for La Rinescente department store in Milan. In 1958, Missoni launched its first eponymous collection that comprised a range of striped shirtdresses. During the early 1960s the couple began experimenting with Raschel knitting machines to produce intricate patterns that would bring them international recognition. During the 1970s Missoni's reputation continued to grow and it diversified into the production of homewares. While the 1990s saw a decline in its popularity, Missoni was firmly back in vogue by the mid-2000s, which led to the increasing diversification of its product lines and well as a successful expansion into the hotel industry.

Issey Miyake
Japanese fashion designer (1938–)
Issey Miyake is well known for his innovative clothing that creatively and imaginatively exploits new technologies and materials. Born in Hiroshima, he studied graphic design at the Tama Art University in Tokyo before working as a fashion designer in Paris and New York. In 1970 he returned to Japan and established the Miyake Design Studio to produce high-end womenswear that was notable for its innovative East-meets-West sensibility. In 1974, he

opened his first shop in Aoyama, Toyko and four years later launched a menswear line. Through the late 1970s and 1980s he opened numerous flagship shops in London, New York and Paris. In the late 1980s he also invented a new method of "memory" pleating, which spawned the launch of his "Pleats Please" brand in 1993. Since then Issey Miyake's fashion empire has expanded to become one of today's most revered clothing brands among the design cognoscenti.

Jean Muir
British fashion designer (1928–95)
Jean Muir preferred to be called a dressmaker rather than a fashion designer and certainly as a child she showed a talent for needlework. Initially working as a sales assistant at Liberty & Co., she later became a designer in the store's ready-to-wear department. In 1956 she moved to Jaeger, where she helped to create the label's "Young Jaeger" fashion range. In 1962, she launched the Jane & Jane label with the backing of the jersey dress manufacturer David Barnes, and two years later won the Dress of the Year award. In 1966 she established Jean Muir Limited with her husband Harry Leukert and continued to produce sensual yet understated clothes that were remarkable for their timeless wearability.

Emilio Pucci
Italian fashion and print designer (1914–92)
Emilio Pucci was a Florentine aristocrat, whose entrée into the fashion world was the result of a ski suit he had designed for a female friend in 1947, a photo of which was featured in *Harper's Bazaar*. He subsequently opened a boutique on the island of Capri in 1950 to sell his exuberantly patterned clothes. From the mid-1960s to the early 1970s he also designed brightly coloured stewardess uniforms for the Braniff airline, which memorably included "Space Bubble" helmets. During the 1970s, Pucci's kaleidoscopically coloured clothes, often made from Emilioform synthetic jersey, as well as his accessories became fashionably *de rigueur* for the international jet set. He was also one of the first designers to diversify into non-fashion products. Today, his eponymous fashion house continues to perpetuate his distinctive "Pucci Look".

Zandra Rhodes
British fashion designer (1940–)
Her mother, who was a fitter for the House of Worth and a lecturer at Medway College of Art, first introduced Zandra Rhodes to world of fashion. Rhodes later studied at Medway College of Art and then went on to train at the Royal College of Art, where she specialized in printed textile design. Because her fabrics were considered far too zany by various British clothing manufacturers, Rhodes began making her own dresses, which led on to her opening a shop in Fulham Road in 1967. Two years later she took her collection to New York, where it was featured in *Vogue*. With her bright pink hair and extrovert personality,

Rhodes was at the forefront of the "new wave" of British fashion during the 1970s and was named Designer of Year in 1972. In 1977, she launched her famous punk-inspired collection, which featured pink and black knitted garments with holes held together with safety pins. In 1997 she received a CBE and in 2003 established the Fashion and Textile Museum in London. Today, Rhodes's designs for clothing and textiles are still sold throughout the world, and she has various licensing agreements for the retail of her non-fashion products.

Mary Quant
British fashion designer (1934–)
Mary Quant studied illustration at Goldsmith's College before landing her first job as a milliner's assistant. In 1955, she opened her own store, Bazaar, on the King's Road and three years later began making clothes to her own design, including very short skirts, which she named after her Mini car. Quant is also often credited with the introduction of coloured tights to match outfits. Her mod-style clothes were central to the Sixties Swinging London scene, and she was the first designer to use PVC as a fashion material. She subsequently launched the Ginger Group to distribute a cheaper diffusion line and in 1966 she introduced a successful cosmetics line. During the late 1960s, Quant also invented another influential if short-lived fashion statement: "hot pants". During the 1970s, her clothing became less girly and more womanly in feel, and therefore more in tune with the fashion trends of the day. During the 1980s she continued to concentrate on her cosmetic and houseware ranges and also published several books on make-up. In 2000 she sold her cosmetics business to a Japanese company, which to this day still bears her iconic flower logo.

Yves Saint Laurent
French fashion designer (1935–2008)
At the age of 17, Yves Saint Laurent left home and moved to Paris in order to work as an assistant to Christian Dior. In 1957, following the death of Christian Dior, he was appointed the House of Dior's designer for Haute Couture. In 1960 he was conscripted for French national service but, unsuited to this life, suffered a nervous breakdown, which led him being released from Dior. In 1962 he went on to found his own YSL label with the backing of his partner, Pierre Bergé. Becoming famous for its "Le Smoking" tuxedos, sheer tops, peasant-style blouses, bolero jackets, Safari jackets and trouser suits, YSL was a trend-setting company which consistently produced stylishly elegant clothing that was beautifully tailored.

Pauline Trigère
French-born American fashion designer (1912–2002)
Pauline Trigère was the daughter of a tailor and after finishing school was employed by the Parisian fashion house Martial et Armand as a trainee cutter. While there, she met the American fashion designer Adèle

Simpson who inspired her to move to New York in 1937. She subsequently worked for Ben Gerschel and Hattie Carnegie, before opening her own fashion house in 1943. Her clothes were beautifully tailored and she also became noted for her design of scarves and jewellery. During the 1970s she created fashions that were often boldly patterned, but which nonetheless retained an element of elegant sophistication.

Emanuel Ungaro
Italian-born French fashion designer (1933–)
The son of an Italian tailor, Emanuel Ungaro moved to Paris in 1955 and three years later began working for Cristobal Balenciaga's fashion house. After three years there, he moved on to work for Courrèges and then in 1965 opened his own fashion studio in Paris with the textile designer Sonja Knapp. As the *Vogue* fashion reporter Jessica Daves noted in 1960, his figure-hugging clothes were "designed for very young women… who are possessed of superb legs and slim, young goddess figures". In 1968, he introduced his ready-to-wear Parallèle line and during the 1970s began creating more loosely fitting fashions. In 1975 he introduced a menswear collection and later in 1991 a sportswear line. In 1996 Ferragamo acquired the Ungaro fashion house.

Valentino
Italian fashion designer (1932–)
Valentino Garavani moved to Paris in 1949, in order to study at the École des Beaux Arts and the Chambre Syndicale de la Couture Parisienne. He subsequently apprenticed at Jean Dessès and later worked for Guy Laroche. He returned to Italy in 1959 and established his own fashion house in Rome. His breakthrough came in 1962 with his first collection shown in Florence, then the Italian fashion capital. He subsequently became a favourite designer of the rich and famous, and by the mid-1960s was widely acknowledged as the maestro of Italian fashion. During the 1970s, he conquered America, spending much of his time in New York socializing with famous personalities from the art and fashion worlds and dressing the city's in-crowd in his elegant gowns. During the 1980s he introduced his first childrenswear collection and in 1989 opened the Academie Valentino cultural centre in Rome. In 1998, he sold his company but stayed on as a designer until 2008.

John Bates (Jean Varon)
British fashion designer (1938–)
John Bates was one of the leading British fashion designers of the 1960s and early 1970s who worked under the *nom-de-plume* "Jean Varon" (from 1959). He created youthful and affordable modernistic clothing, notably see-through Empire-line lace-mesh dresses in the 1960s and brightly coloured flowing garments in the 1970s.

Philippe Venet
French fashion designer (1929–)
Philppe Venet apprenticed as a tailor and later worked from 1951 to 1953 as an assistant designer for Schiaparelli in Paris. He subsequently joined Givenchy as a master tailor in 1953, leaving in 1962 in order to establish his own couture house in Paris. In the 1990s, he diversified into the design of menswear.

Vivienne Westwood
British fashion designer (1941–)
After briefly studying at Harrow School of Art, Vivienne Westwood became a teacher and began making her own jewellery, which she sold from a stall in Portobello Road. In 1971, she gave up teaching in order to open with her lover and business partner Malcolm McLaren a boutique on King's Road, known as "Let It Rock" (renamed "Sex" in 1974). Pioneering a new punk aesthetic in fashion, the pair famously dressed the Sex Pistols in 1976. As punk commercially morphed into the New Romantic style during the early 1980s, Westwood was at the forefront of this new look with her influential "Pirate" collection from 1981. Through the 1980s and 1900s, Westwood's stature grew with her creation of consistently strong-themed collections. In 1990, Westwood expanded into menswear and the following year she was name British Designer of the Year. Today, she is rightly regarded as *the* doyenne of British fashion and is also a prominent ecological campaigner.

INDEX

CREDITS & ACKNOWLEDGEMENTS

The publishers would like to thank the following sources for their kind permission to reproduce the pictures in this book:

Page 3 Getty Images; 4 Condé Nast Archive/Corbis; 7 Getty Images; 12-13 Justin de Villeneuve/Getty Images; 21 Mirrorpix; 25 © Condé Nast Archive/Corbis; 28 Alain Dejean/Sygma/Corbis; 30 Mondadori/Getty Images; 32 Fin Costello/Getty Images; 35 © Condé Nast Archive/ Corbis; 38 © Condé Nast Archive/Corbis; 39 © Condé Nast Archive/Corbis; 41 Hulton Archive/Getty Images; 46 Jamie Hodgson/Getty Images; 47 Jamie Hodgson/Getty Images; 87 Rolls Press/Popperfoto/Getty Images; 96 © Condé Nast Archive/Corbis; 97 © Condé Nast Archive/ Corbis; 99 © Condé Nast Archive/Corbis; 101 © Condé Nast Archive/Corbis; 120-1 Jamie Hodgson/Getty Images; 122 Keystone/Hulton Archive/Getty; 123 Express/ Hulton Archive/Getty; 124 Mirrorpix; 125 Mirrorpix; 142 Archive Photos/Getty Images; 143 H. Armstrong Roberts/ Getty Images; 144 Justin de Villeneuve/Getty Images; 145 Anwar Hussein/Getty Images; 173 © Condé Nast Archive/Corbis; 206 Michael McDonnell/Getty Images; 207 Duffy/Getty Images; 247 Keystone/Hulton Archive/ Getty Images; 260-1 Justin de Villeneuve/Getty Images; 262 Justin de Villeneuve/Getty Images; 263 Justin de Villeneuve/Getty Images; 315 © Condé Nast Archive/ Corbis; 324 Pierre Vauthey/Sygma/Corbis; 336 Mirrorpix; 337 © Condé Nast Archive/Corbis; 358 © Condé Nast Archive/Corbis; 359 © Condé Nast Archive/Corbis; 370 Archive Photos/Getty Images; 371 Slim Aarons/Getty Images; 394-5 Susan Wood/Getty Images; 397 Mirrorpix; 400 Archive Photos/Getty Images; 401 Frederic Lewis/ Getty Images; 404 © Condé Nast Archive/Corbis; 405 © Condé Nast Archive/Corbis.

All other pictures are © Fiell Image Archive 2014. Every effort has been made to acknowledge correctly and contact the source and/or copyright holder of each picture and Carlton Books Limited apologizes for any unintentional errors or omissions, which will be corrected in future editions of this book.